PRAISE FOR *THE FIVE LESSONS*

"As president of the American Medical Association, I've seen firsthand the health risk brought on by debt and poverty. *The Five Lessons* confronts this epidemic head-on with sage advice."

—DR. JOHN NELSON

"This book is a must-read for everyone seeking prosperity through correct financial principles."

—GARY TERAN, president, First Western Advisors

"If married couples learned and used these Five Lessons, money would cease to have the power to control their lives. Instead, it would be their valuable ally in bringing peace and happiness into their family and the world. We highly recommend this amazing book."

—GARY AND JOY LUNDBERG, authors
of the bestselling books *Married for Better, Not Worse* and
I Don't Have to Make Everything All Better

"This book is a blessing. *The Five Lessons* is not only interesting to read, but I firmly believe that it will save many homes and marriages. Every parent should share it with their children and grandchildren. I already have with mine."

—BARBARA SMITH, former president of
American Mothers, Inc.

"The dependence on the illusionary benefits of money is bankrupting the hearts and financial lives of Americans. It is critical that we rethink our beliefs, actions, and relationships with money Is it too late to think differently and make better choices? Evans's answer is a resounding no. The five lessons are a timely blessing that should be instilled into our beliefs and, most importantly, our hearts. I highly recommend everyone read this book."

—BOB BROOKS, *The Prudent Money Show*

"The educational void we have in this country when it comes to money and investing is exposed and examined well in *The Five Lessons*. But Richard Paul Evans makes sure that we don't forget the importance of generosity and kindness to go along with success. . . . This book is a gift of knowledge for anyone looking for the right path to both monetary and spiritual health."

—GARY GOLDBERG, *Money Matters Financial Network*

"This book underscores years of proven lessons I've passed to listeners and clients. I knew it hit the mark after one of my most influential and successful clients called me to say that he passed the book to his grandchildren as a good guide to lessons in life."

—STUART L. STEIN, *Your Estate Matters* radio program

THE FIVE LESSONS

A MILLIONAIRE

TAUGHT ME

ABOUT LIFE

AND WEALTH

Richard Paul Evans

A Fireside Book
Published by Simon & Schuster
New York   London   Toronto   Sydney

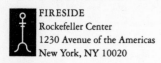
FIRESIDE
Rockefeller Center
1230 Avenue of the Americas
New York, NY 10020

First Fireside Edition 2006

For information regarding special discounts for bulk purchases, please contact Simon &
Schuster Special Sales at 1-800-456-6798 or business@simonandschuster.com.

Designed by Elliott Beard

Manufactured in the United States of America

10   9   8   7

Library of Congress Cataloging-in-Publication Data
Evans, Richard Paul.
    The five lessons a millionaire taught me about life and wealth /
Richard Paul Evans.—1st Fireside ed.
        p.   cm.
    "A Fireside book."
    1. Finance, Personal. 2. Financial security.
HG179.E89 2006   332.024'01—dc22   2005040170

ISBN-13: 978-0-7432-8700-5
ISBN-10:   0-7432-8700-2

To Kerry Heinz, my teacher

In keeping with this book's message,

a portion of the author's profits from this book

will be donated to the Christmas Box Foundation

to help abused and neglected children.

CONTENTS

CONTENTS

FOREWORD

Robert C. Gay

I keep in my office a pair of cowboy boots that once belonged to a business colleague of mine. He had died of cancer, and his wife gave me the boots as a memorial to him. They also serve as a reminder to me of the pitfalls of wealth. This man had built a large company that he had hoped to pass on to his family, but it was not to be. Members of his family derailed that dream with their own ambitions. There was an attempt to wrest control of the company from him through unfriendly means. One of his children ended up in prison for mishandling company funds. What started out as a family dream turned into a nightmare.

This was by no means the first time I had witnessed the deleterious effect of money. My father was the chief executive officer for one of the richest men in the world, Howard Hughes. From this vantage point I saw firsthand the worst aspects of wealth: greedy power struggles, outright deceptions, and even the destruction of souls—all for the sake of money. But perhaps what influenced me most was what I saw in Mr. Hughes himself.

For many years, on Christmas Eve Mr. Hughes would call our home and ask my father to come to work. Then, when my father would arrive, Mr. Hughes would simply say, "Bill, I just wanted to talk." After a couple of hours of friendly conversation, he would say, "It's Christmas. You had better get back to your family." I remember thinking: With all his money and with all his power, he is both lonely and alone.

That experience had a profound effect on me and adversely affected my feelings toward money and wealth. As a young man in my early twenties—while most of my friends were wondering how they would make their first million— I found that my thoughts were elsewhere. I decided that I wanted to be a religion teacher, a social worker, or a psychiatrist—something to help humanity, not destroy it. Truly, I wanted to be anything but a businessperson.

When I went to my dad to discuss my future, I was stunned by his advice. "I think a Harvard MBA would be great for you," he said. I angrily accused him of believing that the only thing in the world that mattered was money. "Son," he replied calmly, "all the love in the world and a few hundred thousand dollars is going to build the next chapel."

With the advantage of twenty-five years of hindsight, I can now see the wisdom of my father's guidance. Through my understanding of money, I have been blessed with the opportunity to be intimately involved in everything my heart desired: poverty elimination, health care, education, youth rehabilitation, and helping to build my church. Through the work of our firm, thousands of jobs have been created and preserved.

I have seen both sides of money, the evil and the sublime. Simply put, wealth without morality is like sex without virtue. The power to procreate is God given and beautiful, but if misused it can bring remarkable pain and tragedy. Likewise, money is a two-edged sword, and has an equal capacity for creating happiness or misery.

As potent as money is, it does not surprise me that most people tend to worship or demonize it. In both cases, they fail to do what they really should be doing: controlling money for the improvement of their own lives and for the betterment of the world. That is why I like *The Five Lessons*. In this book, Richard Paul Evans teaches not only the prudent acquisition of wealth but also the proper mind-set that should accompany that process of acquisition; namely, that money should be controlled for the sake of personal and social good.

The financial principles are true and powerful, and they

work on a small scale as well as a large one. While the principles taught are not new (Evans is the first to admit that they've been passed down and used by successful money managers for centuries), never before have I seen them put together so comprehensively and succinctly, and explained in such a way that nearly anyone can immediately benefit from their practice. *The Five Lessons* is a gift to all those who are wise enough to learn from it. I would as readily recommend this book to the young, cash-strapped newlywed couple as to the manager of a multi-billion-dollar enterprise. I have already instructed my staff to read this book.

What better endorsement could I give than that I plan to share this book with my own children?

Robert C. Gay is a special limited partner and former managing director of Bain Capital, one of the world's leading private investment firms, with over $25 billion in assets under management.

PREFACE

Why I Wrote This Book

I'm frequently asked why a creator of inspirational novels and moral tales would write a book about money. A more appropriate question, I think, is why not? If the intent of my efforts as a writer has been to leave the world a better place, then at no time in history has the message of this book been more relevant or needed.

I believe one of the gravest dangers plaguing modern American culture is fiscal irresponsibility. Never before have so many had so much stuff and so little freedom. Debt is forcing us to work more and more, stealing from us our precious time as well as our happiness. Money problems are breaking our marriages, our homes, and our health, and are a prime motivating factor for crime and domestic abuse. Even the destruction of our environment can be linked to our overconsumption. For millions, debt is turning the American dream into a nightmare.

The Five Lessons contained in this book, if followed, will lead to wealth and financial independence. I know. They've worked in my life. They've worked in my family's lives. And they've worked in the lives of those I've counseled over the last twenty years. But more important than material wealth, these Five Lessons offer freedom in a world increasingly intent on creating financial slavery. *The Five Lessons a Millionaire Taught Me About Life and Wealth* is more than a book—it's the first shot in a revolution aimed at taking back our lives, our homes, and our liberty. I invite you to join our movement.

The gifted man who taught me these principles did so as an act of charity and generosity. I dedicate this book to him.

—*Richard Paul Evans*

THE FIVE LESSONS

A MILLIONAIRE TAUGHT ME

ABOUT LIFE AND WEALTH

INTRODUCTION

The Teacher

**When the student is ready the teacher
shall appear.**

—CHINESE PROVERB

When I was twelve years old, my father, a building contrac-
tor, fell through a stairwell on a construction site and shat-
tered the bones in both of his legs. He had no disability
insurance and no medical insurance, and so the financial result was nothing short of catastrophic. I come from a large
family, and with eight children, money was always tight;
but as my father lay in bed, unable to work for nearly a year,
we were in the direst of circumstances. We were forced to
sell our home and move into a three-bedroom duplex. We
lived off food storage and, to some degree, the generosity of
those around us.

During this difficult time, I had a life-changing experience. One of our neighbors, a very successful businessman
and financial adviser, invited the youth in our area to a lec-

ture at the neighborhood Christian church. He wanted to teach us about money.

We were confident that he knew something about the subject. He owned a professional basketball team, drove an expensive car, and owned buildings and businesses all over the West.

He was also a self-made millionaire. He came from Ashton, Idaho, a tiny farm town with only two thousand residents—"if," he told us, "you count the dogs and chickens." He was born during the Great Depression, and like so many others at that time, his family was destitute. They rented two rooms in the back of someone else's house. They had no running water, and in the freezing northern Idaho climate, the only heat source was the small stove they cooked with. He learned to work as soon as he could walk, toiling as a common laborer picking potatoes on the area farms alongside the migrant workers. He had come a long way since then. He was the wealthiest man I knew.

The first thing he did that day was to pull a hundred-dollar bill from his wallet and hold it up in front of us. I stared at it in wonder. I had never seen one before. He asked, "Is money evil?"

Even though it was an evil we all wanted, sitting in the confines of a church we all quickly agreed that it was.

"The Bible," said a teenage girl piously, "says that money is the root of all evil."

He smiled. "You are referring to the New Testament scripture in 1 Timothy, chapter 6, verse 10," he replied. "And it does not say that. It says that *the love of money* is the root of all evil. There's a big difference. In fact, just one chapter earlier in Timothy, the apostle Paul says that if 'any provide not for his own, he hath denied the faith, and is worse than an infidel.' How can you provide for your own without money?

"How about the parable of the Good Samaritan? Jesus told us to be like the Good Samaritan, yet how many of you here today could afford to pay for a stranger's hospital treatment and housing for a week? The Samaritan was able to help because he had the financial means to do so. Without it he could only have offered minor assistance.

"For many, religion seems paradoxical on the subject of wealth. On the one hand, it seems to tell us that money is evil. On the other hand, God often blesses the righteous with wealth and material prosperity. For instance, in the Old Testament, after Job endured his many trials and proved his devotion to God, he was given back twice his wealth and possessions. So was God rewarding Job's righteousness with evil? Of course not."

Our teacher's tone became more serious. "Like most

things, money can be used for good or evil. The church you are sitting in right now was built through substantial monetary contributions. Every week I see people in our area being helped through the generosity and financial ability of others.

"At your age, you have no idea how much money is spent on your behalf—oftentimes by people you will never meet and never thank. The day will come when you must make a decision: will you be one who helps others or one who looks to others for help? It's your choice. You can be part of the problem or part of the solution. If you want to be the latter, then listen carefully, because what I have to tell you today will change your life."

Considering my family's plight at the time, I listened *very* carefully. The lessons he taught that day lit a flame of hope within me. For the first time, I believed that there might be more to life than the seemingly endless financial desperation that had been my family's lot. I thought about his words constantly and began living the principles he shared. I immediately saw a difference in my own life, and that made the belief burn still brighter. By the age of sixteen, I had become somewhat financially independent. I bought my own clothes, my own car, and paid for my own entertainment. By eighteen, I had saved the equivalent of

$7,000, enough to finance my schooling and a church mission. By the age of twenty-six, I had saved enough to put 25 percent down on a house on a beautiful tree-lined street. By the age of thirty-one, I had paid off my home.

Less than twenty years from the time my millionaire friend gave that talk, I returned to him with several million dollars I wanted his help in investing. He smiled when he saw me. "I understand that you've done all right for yourself."

"I have you to thank," I said. "You taught me what it takes to succeed financially."

"You have yourself to thank," he replied. Then his smile turned to a look of concern. "I'm afraid you were the only one who listened to me that day."

"Maybe I was just the only one who thought he had to."

THE MILLIONAIRE IN THE MIRROR

Why is it that wealth seems so distant from most people? Recently my eight-year-old daughter asked my wife if she'd ever seen a millionaire. My wife smiled and said that she had.

"Was he wearing a crown?" she asked.

"No."

"Was he in a limousine?"

"No, he was just walking."

"Were people dancing around him saying, 'Go million-aire, go millionaire?'"

Millionaires are not as removed as you might think. There are more than three and a half *million* millionaires in the United States alone. In fact, if you have an average American's income, you will earn more than a million dollars in your lifetime. So will you someday be a millionaire? According to current financial trends, it's not likely.

Recent statistics given by the Federal Reserve indicate that household debt is at a record high relative to disposable income. In 1946, household debt was 22 percent of personal disposable income. Today it's roughly 110 percent. Not surprisingly, personal bankruptcies in America have more than doubled in the last decade. In fact, more Americans now declare bankruptcy each year than graduate from college.

What about our retirement? If we take one hundred Americans and follow their financial path to age sixty-five, fewer than four will have an income above $35,000, while five times that number will live below the poverty line. More than 50 percent will be wholly dependent on relatives, Social Security, and welfare. In America, the discrepancy between the haves and have-nots has never been so wide.

If Americans' individual financial prospects seem so dire, then who and where are these millions of millionaires?

They are not all businesspeople, doctors, lawyers, or white-collar professionals. Some are hairstylists and welders and farmers. So what's their secret? What is it that makes these people wealthy and others not?

IS IT LUCK?

> "Fickle fate" is a vicious Goddess who brings no permanent good to anyone. On the contrary, she brings ruin to almost every man upon whom she showers unearned gold. She makes wanton spenders who soon dissipate all they receive and are left beset by overwhelming appetites and desires they have not the ability to gratify.
> —George S. Clason, *The Richest Man in Babylon*

Wealth is more than just luck. Only 2 percent of today's millionaires inherited all or any part of their homes or property. Fewer than 20 percent inherited even a small portion of their wealth. And those victims of luck-induced wealth don't often retain their prizes. One study showed that of those who came into fortunes through lotteries, more than 80 percent were bankrupt within five years. The fate of those receiving other windfalls, such as insurance claims and inheritance, isn't much better.

IS IT INTELLIGENCE?

If wealth were simply a matter of intelligence, a disproportionate number of millionaires would have stellar IQs and academic merit badges. This is not the case. Most of today's millionaires did not graduate with high honors. Most of them did not even qualify for a top-rated college. In light of this, it is not surprising, then, that Warren Buffett, the self-made multibillionaire investor, was rejected by Harvard Business College. In fact, research shows that millionaires' average grade point average is lower than a B.

On the other hand, highly academic, well-educated people often act like complete fools when it comes to personal finances. It is common knowledge among financial consultants that America's most educated citizens—doctors and lawyers—are notoriously bad at handling their money.

WHAT IS IT?

If it's not luck or superior intelligence that makes the millionaire, then what is the common denominator (besides money, of course) that the wealthy have and the rest of humanity does not? It's simply this:

The wealthy understand the principles of accumulating wealth and live them.

Some wealthy people learned the principles of accumulating riches through trial and error. Some—like myself—learned from mentors or parents. And for some, it just came naturally. But whatever this knowledge's source, I do not know a single self-made millionaire who does not understand and apply the five principles my millionaire friend taught us that day.

This is good news for everyone else. Because it means that wealth is less a matter of circumstance than it is a matter of knowledge and choice. It means that we can choose to live the lives we desire. So ultimately it comes back to you. Where do you want to go?

LESSON ONE

Decide to Be Wealthy

"Would you tell me, please," Alice asked, "which way I ought to go from here?"

"That depends a good deal on where you want to get to," said the Cat.

"I don't much care where—" said Alice.

"Then it doesn't matter which way you go," said the Cat.

"—so long as I get *somewhere*," Alice added as an explanation.

"Oh, you're sure to do that," said the Cat, "if you only walk long enough."

—LEWIS CARROLL, *Alice's Adventures in Wonderland*

WHO WANTS TO BE A MILLIONAIRE?

Heather and James sat across from me in the Japanese restaurant, hopeless, irritable, and visibly upset. They couldn't figure out what had gone wrong. They had increased their income by nearly 35 percent in the last year, but were further in debt than ever before. They couldn't figure out how their expenses had increased so dramatically, or how their life had gotten so out of control. Now it looked like things were going to get worse. Their car, which they had just refinanced to cover credit card debt, was on the verge of breaking down. They had already taken a second mortgage on their home and were now looking at refinancing their home to meet their rocketing debt. Stress was at an all-time high, and they had been fighting a lot.

"What do you want from life?" I asked.

"Not this," Heather replied cynically.

"You make a lot of money," I said. "In fact, together you'll earn close to four million dollars by the time you retire."

They looked at me in disbelief.

"Do the math," I said. "Unfortunately, with your current lifestyle you'll be bankrupt in less than two years."

Heather shook her head. "If not sooner."

"If you really want to change, I can help. But you need to do something first."

"What's that?"

"I want you to decide to be wealthy."

"Wealthy?" Heather said. "Out of debt would be nice."

"It's a mind-set," I said. "It's all or nothing."

"Wealthy sounds good to me," James said.

"Wait a minute," Heather said. "Does this mean that we have to live in poverty for the next twenty years? Because I don't think I can do that."

"Not at all. In fact, the beauty of this program is that you won't really miss anything."

"How is that possible?"

"Trust me. I started doing this decades ago. But remember, it's all or nothing. If you can't decide, then I'd rather not waste our time."

"I'm in," James said.

"Me too," Heather said.

"Then let's get started."

For the next hour I shared with them the Five Lessons I'd learned years before from my millionaire friend. At the end of the hour, we sat over empty plates in a nearly empty restaurant.

"So what do you think?" I asked.

"I feel hope again," James said.

"We can do this," Heather said.

"I know you can. Anyone can. If they'll just decide that's what they want." I picked up the check. "And don't worry, I'll pay for dinner. You can buy next time."

Fifteen months later, we met again. Same restaurant, same city, different world.

"So tell me, how are things?"

Heather was all smiles. "Not only have we paid off all of our debt, but we've saved more than thirty thousand dollars. I also bought a new wardrobe, and took an incredible trip to Italy I couldn't possibly have afforded before."

"It doesn't sound like you've had to cut back on your standard of living."

"Cut back? We've given up a few things, but all in all, it's never been so good. Especially if you consider that we don't fight over money anymore. And our kids have lost weight since we stopped eating junk food every night. This last Christmas was great. It was the first time we didn't use our credit cards and, frankly, we bought more for our kids than ever. I'm the happiest"—she stopped and looked fondly at her husband—"we're the happiest we've been in years. We work together and we have more than we've ever had."

James nodded in agreement. "Life is so much better. I can even envision a time when I'll be able to help others financially."

They looked at each other and smiled.

"Any regrets?" I asked.

"Only one," Heather said. "I wish that we'd started ten years earlier."

This time they paid for dinner.

Life isn't about money. It's about God. It's about love. It's about family and relationships. It's about personal evolution, learning, and growth.

Part of that growth is learning balance between the different forces of life. Money, like health and spirituality, is part of that symmetry, and for those who do not accept responsibility for financial matters, life is thrown out of balance. As a dentist friend once told me: "Those who don't think about their teeth are those who later in life spend the most time thinking about them." It's no different with money.

It's not surprising, then, that the people I know who are the most obsessed with money are not the millionaires or even the billionaires. Rather, the most obsessed with money are the ones who are living paycheck to paycheck. To the financially enslaved, life becomes all about money. It's not.

In order to be truly happy, we must live balanced lives. To be in great fiscal health is very much like being in great physical health: it allows you to do more and be more, and it permits you to live your life free of constant pain and bondage.

Money is a powerful ally. With money I've been able to provide life's necessities for my family and loved ones: food, comfortable shelter, as well as superior education and medical care. I've been able to retire my parents. I've provided jobs and income for others. I've helped friends in tough circumstances. I've been able to build shelters to help abused children and support other worthy causes all around the world. It has also allowed my family and me to see the world. Wealth has brought freedom of choice and opportunity.

Lack of money is the root of all evil.

—GEORGE BERNARD SHAW

On the other hand, the cost of financial distress is astronomical. The American Bar Association has indicated that nearly 90 percent of all divorces over the last decade can be traced to quarrels and accusations over money. Some marriage experts have estimated that 75 percent of all divorces result directly from clashes over finances.

Debt and poverty contribute to other serious social issues, as well. Studies by the Children's Welfare League of America have demonstrated a direct correlation between financial problems and domestic abuse.

And there's more bad news for the fiscally challenged. Numerous studies have shown the connection between debt and disease. One study published in the *Journal of Law, Medicine and Ethics* found that "nearly half the debtors reported that debt troubles had affected their health."

In the end, what *wealthy* means is up to you. To me,

when you no longer have to think about money, then you are truly wealthy.

The good news is that, for the most part, whether to be wealthy or not is ultimately your choice. As my millionaire friend said, you can either become part of the problem or part of the solution. That is the first lesson I learned. My life changed the day he taught me about wealth, because that was the day I decided to be wealthy.

EXTRAVAGANT ≠ WEALTHY?

> The most substantial people are the most frugal and make the least show, and live at the least expense.
>
> — FRANCES MOORE

Before you make the life-changing decision to be wealthy, you must discard whatever media-engendered notions you may have acquired concerning what it means to be rich. From a public relations standpoint, America's wealthy need an image remake. They are too often stereotyped as having gaudy, extravagant lifestyles and irresponsible fiscal habits. The media perpetuates this caricature by focusing on the small percentage of wealthy individuals who do live such ostentatious lives: *Lifestyles of the Rich and Famous* wannabes. While such people do exist, they are the exception, not the rule.

Two groundbreaking books have done much to shed light on the reality of America's millionaires. In *The Millionaire Next Door* by Thomas J. Stanley, PhD, and William D. Danko, PhD, and *The Millionaire Mind* by Thomas J. Stanley, PhD, these scholars reveal that today's millionaires are remarkably frugal and careful with their money. In fact, in many cases even their own children do not know of their wealth.

Living lives of excess, exorbitance, and waste are counter to the message of this book. And, as I discuss later, such overindulgence is often short-lived. Most people you see trying to look wealthy are doing just that. An expensive car or home does not make one wealthy. In fact, the inverse is more likely true. The path I'm recommending teaches individuals how to achieve a real and enduring affluent lifestyle based on spiritual and life-centered values.

THE POWER OF COMMITMENT

As simple as this First Lesson seems, it is my experience that it is the primary reason most people fail to achieve wealth. They simply never decide to be wealthy.

Choice is the beginning of all journeys. And, as with all first steps, it is the most important step of all. It is also the easiest. As Napoleon Hill wrote in his classic book, *Think and Grow Rich*:

"Riches begin with a state of mind, with defi-
niteness of purpose, with little or no hard work."

There is something remarkably powerful about commitment. Commitment to a plan or thought carries with it
a force that can influence the unconscious mind and bring
about the desired effect. In other words, once we decide to
have something, the mind unconsciously begins to create
the reality necessary to bring to pass what we desire. The
opposite is true as well. If we believe that we can't do
something, we can't. If we think we will fail, most likely
we will.

To illustrate the unseen power of commitment, try this
simple experiment. Take a piece of string and tie it to a key.
Hold one end of the string with your clenched fist, dan-
gling the key in front of you. Now look at the key and men-
tally tell it to rotate clockwise. Don't move your fist; just
watch the key. It will begin to move in the direction you
desire. Then desire the key to stop. Then tell it to change its
direction to rotate counterclockwise.

The key's movement seems almost mystical. But what
you are really seeing is your body moving in almost imper-
ceptible ways to grant your desire. What you have desired
to happen is, in fact, happening.

ASK AND YOU WILL RECEIVE

I believe the power of desire has even greater, spiritual implications. About fifteen years ago I had the desire to travel to China. I didn't have sufficient funds at the time to justify such an expensive trip, but I wrote my desire down on a list of goals for the year. Four months later, a friend called me out of the blue. She had just won an all-expenses-paid trip to China for two. Her husband didn't really want to go, so she asked if my wife and I would like to take the trip instead. Of course you could call that a coincidence, but the odds of something like that happening would suggest otherwise.

TO CHOOSE THE PATH IS
TO CHOOSE THE DESTINATION

After one of my seminars, a man approached me. "Your presentation was insightful, but you're wrong on one point," he said. "I've never decided to be a millionaire. But I am."

"How did you become a millionaire?" I asked.

He thought about it. "Well, pretty much by living the other four lessons you taught tonight."

"Let me ask you this: if you decide to live a healthy lifestyle, are you in fact deciding to be healthy?"

"Probably. Yes."

"Exactly. You decided to be wealthy when you decided to live the principles of accumulating wealth."

He smiled. "I guess I did decide."

ONE SMALL STEP

It's within your power, right now, to take the first step to wealth. Decide to be wealthy. Declare your intention by saying it out loud, then writing on a card:

Today I decide to be wealthy.

Put that card in a nightstand or next to your toothbrush. Look at it and read those words every morning when you get up and every evening when you go to bed. Keep a copy of it in your wallet next to your credit card. Do this for the next two months.

Then congratulate yourself. You've just made a life-changing decision.

LESSON ONE

Decide to Be Wealthy

LESSON TWO

Take Responsibility for Your Money

Money makes a good servant but a bad master.

— FRENCH PROVERB

When it comes to money, far too many of us are asleep at the wheel. Many Americans view money as an uncontrollable, almost mystical entity. It's not. In its most basic form, it's just metal and paper. And if you don't control your money, it will control you.

Taking control of your money begins with taking responsibility for it. That means knowing how much you have, where it is coming from, where it is going, and what it's doing in the meantime. Taking responsibility for your money means not completely turning it over to a bookkeeper or a spouse. It's a matter of personal stewardship. It's like parenting: you cannot leave control of your children to someone else and just hope that they will turn out all right.

It's not just the poor or uneducated who fall prey to fiscal irresponsibility. An acquaintance of mine with more than ten million dollars to his name woke one day to find himself nearly broke. The group of investors he had hired to manage his money had tied it up in risky investments that had not only wiped out his capital but left major debts in excess of what he owned. He had been too busy in other ventures to watch where his money was going.

Another acquaintance, finding his bank account depleted after burning through tens of thousands of dollars, said to me, "We have nothing to show for it. All I can figure out is that we spent all our money on Happy Meals."

Unfortunately, most people's closets are more organized than their finances. If you're one of the fiscally irresponsible, it's time for change.

A NEW BEGINNING

No matter how irresponsible you've been in the past, or still are, it's never too late to take control. These are the four steps to taking responsibility for your money.

1. KNOW HOW MUCH MONEY YOU HAVE

How much are you really worth? The Net Worth form in the back of this book will help you calculate your current monetary value and will give you a starting point for your wealth accumulation.* Think of it as stepping on a scale at the start of a diet.

At the end of each month, fill out the report again to chart your progress. Then, at the end of each year, fill out an annual report. This will give you the most accurate view of your accumulating wealth. As your wealth grows, you'll find yourself looking forward to completing the forms.

2. KNOW WHERE YOUR MONEY COMES FROM

Every paycheck, bonus, interest payment, alimony check, child-support payment, royalty, dividend, gift, and tip you receive should be recorded on a ledger as income. This information will help you in two ways. First, it will clarify how your time is best used to increase your income.

For instance, a while back I decided to try breaking into the music-production business. I started with one artist, a talented, locally popular musician. His CD was successful and even hit the national billboard charts; but when we completed reviewing our annual income, we learned that what took 30 to 40 percent of my time actually brought in

---

* Additional forms and a Net Worth Calculator are available free of charge on our Web site at: thefivelessons.com.

less than 1 percent of my income. I quickly got out of the business and focused my attention on other areas that were more profitable.

Second, knowing where your money comes from will help you decide how your money should be used. Ongoing income, such as your monthly salary, and alimony or child-support payments, should cover ongoing expenditures. One-time money, such as a bonus or inheritance, should be used to pay for one-time expenditures, such as a vacation or an education fund, or for paying down your mortgage.

3. KNOW WHERE YOUR MONEY IS GOING

While it is useful and important to know what you are worth and where your money comes from, understanding exactly where you are spending your money is the only way to gain control of it. You can't plug the holes in your boat if you don't know where they are.

As my own financial empire grew, I became careless and relinquished more and more control to others. I soon found myself running short on cash. When I regained control of my finances, I discovered that my overhead had nearly doubled in my absence.

For tracking your spending, I recommend the use of a checkbook and a simple computer program such as

Quicken. But technology is not necessary. For the first twenty years of my financial life, I kept track of my money in an inexpensive ledger I purchased at an office supply store. In the Resources section at the end of this book is a Cash Flow form. This form will help you categorize all your income and expenses. You will notice that the first line under "Expenditures" is for documenting how much you are paying yourself. In the next lesson you will learn to always keep a portion of what you earn.

The second expenditure on the form is for charitable donations. Lesson Five addresses this important budget item. The rest of your expense categories will depend on your lifestyle. Each expenditure on your Cash Flow form has the opportunity for reduction. To help you maximize your income, I've compiled a tip sheet on ways to comfortably cut down on expenses in each spending category (see "Winning in the Margins with Savings" in the Resources section of this book).

MORE THAN YOU THINK

As you track your money, you will quickly discover that most things cost more than you think. For instance, a friend of mine wanted to buy a new car. It was an expensive car, more than $30,000, and would require her to sacrifice to afford it. It didn't sound like a good idea to me, and I told her so.

"But we can make the payments," she countered.

"Wouldn't you be just as happy with a car in the twenty-thousand-dollar range?" I asked.

She thought about it. "But I want *that* car. And we can afford it."

"Are you sure? Have you considered all the costs?"

"It's just $240 more a month than my last car."

"How much are the extra taxes?"

"I hadn't thought about that."

"How about the extra insurance?"

"I don't know. I hadn't thought about that either."

She looked up the additional expenses—and found that they came to almost a thousand dollars a year.

"So you're paying almost an additional four thousand dollars a year for this car. Add another ten percent for lost interest on that money. And since this SUV is not as fuel efficient as your current car, add another five hundred dollars a year. You're now up to almost five thousand dollars. With state and federal taxes, how much extra do you need to earn to bring home that much?"

"I don't know. About seven thousand."

"So you just took a seven-thousand-dollar pay decrease in order to drive a more expensive new car that you probably won't care that much about six months from now."

After realizing the actual cost involved, she decided against the purchase.

• • •

Learning where your money is going is the most important step to gaining control of your finances. It is also an important way to gain control of your life.

A woman I know, frustrated that her money was always running short each month, finally took all her financial records to a CPA to see if he could make sense of them. He found large discrepancies in the records, and it was only then that she discovered that her husband had a drug problem.

4. KNOW WHAT YOUR MONEY IS DOING

The entire point of amassing wealth is to make it work for you. Eventually, as you stay true to yourself and the Five Lessons, your money will earn more each year than your salary. Money will become your servant instead of the other way around. If you had an employee who sat around and did nothing, you would quickly fire him. Ongoing, monthly evaluation of your investments is vital to your financial success. As you fill out your monthly Net Worth form, you will see clearly just how hard your money is working for you.

Exactly where you should put your money to make it work for you is a much more complex matter and is addressed more fully in the next lesson.

"I don't have time for this . . ."

Saying that you don't have time to follow your money is like saying that you don't have time to watch the traffic signals as you drive. In fact, you don't have time not to. You spend thousands of hours each year earning—why wouldn't you take a few hours a month to track where it goes?

"There are none so blind as those who will not see," the saying goes. It's time to open your eyes. Ultimately, it is the only rational way to live.

LESSON TWO

Take Responsibility for Your Money

LESSON THREE

Keep a Portion of Everything You Earn

You can't touch this.

—M. C. HAMMER

News stories about celebrities declaring bankruptcy or crying to the media about their financial woes never cease to amaze me. From rock stars pawning their Grammys in order to pay delinquent tax bills to former professional boxers waiting on tables, the list of financial casualties grows annually.

The questions I find myself asking are, Why didn't they just put some of what they had someplace safe? Why didn't they save the proceeds from just one album or, in the case of the boxer, just one title fight? If they had, they'd still be wealthy.

IT'S NOT JUST THE CELEBRITIES

Of course, celebrities aren't the only ones making bad financial choices. A financial adviser told me the tragic story of a client who had been seriously injured at work, losing a limb in an on-the-job accident. In compensation, he had received a $3 million insurance settlement—enough, if properly handled, to enable him to support his family indefinitely at a level significantly higher than what they were used to.

Almost immediately after my friend created a financial plan for this couple, their resolve to responsibly manage their wealth weakened. Seduced by their sudden riches, they began taking a little here and there, buying things, recklessly loaning money to family and friends, launching unwise business ventures—the list of expenses grew as their account diminished. On a subsequent meeting with this couple, my friend noticed that the woman was wearing the largest diamond he had ever seen. "She deserves it," her husband said, "after all she's been through with my accident."

In spite of my friend's ongoing counsel and encouragement, week after week the couple withdrew funds until, less than three years later, they were completely broke and were both out looking for work.

The reason they and others in similar situations fail is twofold. First, because of a dangerous mind-set—the erroneous belief that they can always make more. Then they suffer that first downturn in sales or their first knockdown, and their financial house of cards collapses. Second, and more importantly, it's because they do not understand the principles of wealth, especially the Third Lesson: A portion of all you earn is yours to keep.

"But *all* I earn is mine to keep," you might reply.

If that's true, then why do you have so little of it left? The truth is that you give your money to everyone *but* yourself.

You've heard it said before and it's true: "It's not what you earn; it's what you *keep* that makes you rich." The wealthy person pays herself first.

"Pay yourself first" is a popular modern financial catchphrase, but it has actually been around for decades. Back in the twenties, George S. Clason wrote:

"I found the road to wealth when I decided that a part of all I earned was mine to keep."

How much should you pay yourself? "That depends a good deal," as the Cheshire Cat said to Alice, "on where you want to get to." And how fast you want to get there. Obviously, the more you put away, the faster you'll achieve your goal. I recommend that you push yourself as hard as possible at first—just to test your limits. Then, when you ease back, you will find your comfort zone. However, the amount you save should be *a minimum of 10 percent of your on-going salary and 90 to 100 percent of your side earnings.* Research shows that most American millionaires save between 15 and 20 percent of their incomes.

THE POWER OF COMPOUND INTEREST

You may have heard the joke about Einstein dying and going to heaven. While they were putting the final touches on his heavenly mansion, he was temporarily placed in an apartment with three roommates. His first roommate had an IQ of 180.

"Great," Einstein exclaimed. "We can talk about the theory of relativity."

The second roommate had an IQ of 140. "Good," Einstein said. "We can talk about Mensa."

The third roommate had an IQ of 75. "Okay," he said. "We'll talk about interest rates."

As simple as interest is to understand, the majority of Americans do not realize the power of compounding interest until it is too late to take full advantage of it. The following tables illustrate the power of compound interest. According to the 2000 census, the average American household's income is $46,805 a year.

If Mr. and Mrs. Average allocate 10 (or 15 or 20) percent
of their income to their nest egg and earn an average interest rate of 10.2 percent (based on the average S&P 500 over
the last fifty years) they will accumulate wealth at the following rates:

10%		15%		20%	
Year	Savings	Year	Savings	Year	Savings
1	**$5,158**	1	**$7,737**	1	**$10,316**
5	**$31,615**	5	**$47,423**	5	**$63,230**
10	**$82,996**	10	**$124,494**	10	**$165,993**
15	**$166,501**	15	**$249,752**	15	**$333,002**
20	**$302,214**	20	**$453,320**	20	**$604,427**
30	**$881,230**	30	**$1,321,845**	30	**$1,762,459**
40	**$2,410,579**	40	**$3,615,868**	40	**$4,821,157**

Years until achieving
the first million:
around 32.

Years until achieving
the first million:
around 28.

Years until achieving
the first million:
around 25.

And it gets even better. Lesson Four describes a method
that allows you to more than double these amounts.

"I can't save that much . . ."

Initially, putting 10 percent of your income into your nest egg might require some faith. But it's worth the leap. Prove it for yourself. I've heard it over and over again from those who've tried: "We never missed the money we put away."

This program isn't about deprivation. I've found that most people I interview are losing between 10 and 20 percent of their income. That is, that much of their income disappears without a trace. This being the case, I tell them the good news about their dilemma: they can easily save and invest that much of their income and not notice any change in their current lifestyle. In fact, as was earlier illustrated by Heather and James's situation, most of those I've helped have actually experienced an improvement in their standard of living. As they adhere to the Five Lessons, they find themselves managing the remaining percentage of their income much better than before.

STARTING YOUR NEST EGG

Becoming wealthy is as much a psychological and emotional exercise as a physical one. Anyone who has ever dieted knows that it's easier to stick to a diet when you see immediate progress in the mirror and on the scale. Likewise, the most powerful way to encourage new, wealth-accumulating behavior is to see visible, tangible results. I found that the best way to see tangible results is to create tangible wealth—to have something you can watch grow. In fiscal terms, this is called a nest egg:

A sum of money put aside for future expenses.

Personally, I prefer the dictionary's older, original definition of a nest egg:

A real or artificial egg that is put in a hen's nest to encourage it to continue laying after the other eggs have been removed.

This definition alludes to a powerful psychological need for anyone attempting to accumulate wealth: the provision of incentives in order to spur further productivity. I cannot overstate the importance of creating an abiding mental concept of your nest egg.

When I was fourteen years old, I decided to start building my wealth by collecting precious metals. I couldn't afford gold coins, but silver was selling for around three dollars an ounce—about two hours of work at my part-time job. I took one of my mom's canning jars and began filling it with one-ounce silver rounds. This method of wealth accumulation had several advantages. First, the fact that the rounds were not actual currency lessened the temptation to spend them. If I wanted to, I would first have to cash them in at a coin shop and take a loss in doing so.

Second, I could actually see myself growing richer. As a poor boy, I found it satisfying to watch my wealth increase and, as nothing fuels success like success, the desire to watch the pile of silver grow helped motivate me to save more. The coins multiplied quickly, and soon I had filled several jars. Then I filled an entire wooden chest with silver. I felt like a pirate with a treasure chest. By the time I was eighteen, I had saved thousands of dollars.

James and Heather chose to follow the precious metals route as well. Heather pointed out to me two advantages she had discovered in accumulating metals. First, it gave her perspective. She began to weigh the cost of an item against the price of silver. For example, she said, "I could take my kids out for dinner or I could buy four more pieces of silver."

Second, purchasing the silver rounds satisfied Heather's urge to spend. Like so many others, she had discovered that she was a shopaholic—so spending her money on silver was like eating her cake and having it too.

PURCHASING PRECIOUS METALS

As with all investments, there are pros and cons to purchasing precious metals. Starting your nest egg with precious metals is good for emotional and security reasons, but in the long run, it is not likely to pay out the interest you need for steady financial growth. In the last fifty years, the average annual return on precious metals has been around 4½ percent—less than half the rate of return of the S&P 500. For this reason, I recommend starting your nest egg with metals; then, after the first year, enlist the help of a professional financial adviser and turn to other forms of investments.

If you're on a limited income, I recommend purchasing silver. I began with .999 pure one-ounce silver rounds as opposed to coins or bullion. You'll pay a bit more for rounds, but they offer a better guarantee of authenticity, and you'll recover the extra money paid when you sell. Be careful not to buy (unless it's your intention) special collector's coins, as they likewise carry a special price, which may not be recoverable when it comes time to sell.

The same is true if you're purchasing gold. For gold, .999 pure one-ounce coins (as well as other weights) are minted in the form of Canadian Maple Leafs, American Eagles, and South African Krugerrands.

Both silver and gold are available at coin shops and precious metal dealers. Be sure to shop around before you purchase, as dealers update their prices at different times of the day.

SEEK PROFESSIONAL ASSISTANCE

Ultimately, how and where you keep your nest egg is a decision you should base on your own current financial needs and the availability of trustworthy financial counsel.

As your investment builds, take the time to learn more about investing and investment opportunities. Diversity is important. As your nest egg grows, you may want to have a combination of securities, precious metals, and real estate. A 401(k) can be a very powerful tool in building wealth. Above all, avoid risky schemes and investments, no matter the supposed payoff. Just as you would consult a doctor before making any serious decisions regarding your health, consult an established, successful investment counselor before you make any major investment decision.

DON'T KILL THE GOOSE THAT LAYS THE GOLDEN EGGS

As you watch your nest egg grow, you will begin to feel the power that comes from wealth. You will notice things that are within your financial grasp that were not available to you before. With this newfound power you will be tempted to dip into the nest and steal a few eggs. Resist. Most of us are familiar with the fable "The Goose That Laid the Golden Eggs." In this story, a poor country man discovers that one of his geese lays golden eggs—but only one a day. At first, he is happy with his newfound riches. But as his wealth grows, he becomes greedy and impatient. Finally, he decides to cut the goose open to get all the gold at once. Of course, in so doing he only manages to kill the goose and gets no more eggs.

This is exactly how you must view your nest egg. In time it will earn more income than you can by working full-time—but only if you leave it alone long enough to allow it to grow.

SHOULD I FIRST PAY OFF MY DEBT?

What to do with current debt is a question that most face as they gain control of their money. Should you first pay off your debt? The unequivocal answer is: it depends. The first thing I recommend is that you consolidate your debt with the lowest interest rate possible. If you are struggling with significant debt, you might want to consult with a CCCS, a consumer credit counseling service.

This is the time to perform what author and radio personality Dave Ramsey calls "plastic surgery." Cut up your credit cards. One of the worst things that could happen after you have consolidated your debt is for you to create a new form of debt.

With a debt-repayment plan in place, consider the amount of interest you're paying and decide if eliminating your debt first is the right thing to do.

In most cases, I recommend using 10 percent of your funds for debt repayment and 10 percent for your wealth accumulation, even if you are losing a few percentage points in interest. The reason for this is psychological. It is important, emotionally, for you to see the growth of your wealth. If you're not seeing your wealth increase, you will be less motivated and, ultimately, less likely to succeed.

There is another advantage to simultaneously saving and paying off your debt. It will help train your new lifestyle. Once your debt is paid off, apply the extra 10 percent to your nest egg to accelerate your wealth accumulation.

LESSON THREE

Keep a Portion of Everything You Earn

 **LESSON FOUR**

Win in the Margins

Fortune befriends the bold.

— VIRGIL, *The Aeneid,* TRANSLATED
BY JOHN DRYDEN

Of all the lessons, Lesson Four has the most to do with the speed of my own financial success. What does it mean to win in the margins? Simply this: *The wealthy find additional ways to increase contributions to their growing nest egg.*

J. Paul Getty, once named the richest man in the world by *Fortune* magazine, called this "the Millionaire Mentality":

> "The Millionaire Mentality watches costs and tries to reduce them—and strives to increase production and sales and thus profits."

Though Getty was speaking specifically about business, the principles are true in all areas of finance. There are essentially two ways to win in the margins. The first is by earning extra income. The second is by keeping more of what you earn. I recommend that you do both.

WINNING IN THE MARGINS WITH EXTRA INCOME

I once had a friend who had the peculiar habit of looking for money. He would actually walk or ride his bike while looking down. As odd as his behavior was, the most surprising result of his habit was that nearly every day he would find something. We would be walking along when suddenly he'd stop, bend over, and lift a coin or bill from the ground. I'm not recommending that you start walking looking down. My point in sharing this story is to demonstrate that you find what you are looking for. When you start looking for ways to increase your income, you will discover that there are opportunities all around you that you have never thought of or noticed. The following examples illustrate this principle.

COFFEE CANS OF GOLD

My wife's grandfather, Pietro Disera, emigrated from Italy to America when he was only seventeen. He came west looking for work and found employment in the gold and silver mines of the Tintic mining area west of the Salt Lake Valley. He worked the night shift at the furnaces where the processed ore was smelted in order to separate the gold from the other metals before being poured into bullion. Pietro noticed that the gold would occasionally explode, splashing the metal inside on the hood of the small furnace. He asked his foreman if he could keep the metal he found if he stayed after his shift and cleaned the hood on his own time. The foreman agreed.

At the end of each shift, Pietro would climb into the furnace and scrape the thin gold flakes from the metal hood into an empty coffee can. Within months, the poor immigrant boy had collected two coffee cans filled to the brim with the precious metal—nearly twenty pounds of gold.

SCRAP WOOD

Clinton Phelps grew up in the wooded mountains of southern Oregon. To provide for his family, he drove a truck, hauling lumber from a nearby lumber mill. While waiting for his truck to be loaded, he often heard the mill workers complain about the mill's waste products. After the usable wood was cut into boards, the remaining slabs were thrown on a conveyor belt and transported to an incinerator to be burned. Much of the wood was too green to burn well, and the mill workers had trouble keeping up with the waste. In addition, the smoke from the incinerator had the townspeople and environmentalists constantly up in arms.

One day, Clinton had an idea. He asked the mill owners if they would allow him to take the wood, offering to cut it up and haul it away at no charge to them. Glad to be free of the problem, they accepted his offer—even agreeing to pay for the electricity he needed to cut the wood. Before long, he was hauling out nearly one hundred cords of firewood every day, which he sold in a nearby town.

He may have been just a truck driver with an eighth-grade education, but with a simple idea he had increased his salary by more than a hundred thousand dollars a year. And the land he bought years ago to store the wood is now worth millions.

RENTING FARMLAND

Warren Buffett, the sagacious multibillionaire, learned the lesson of winning in the margins early in life. At the age of just fourteen he bought forty acres of Nebraska farmland with money he made on his paper route and then rented the land. He also invested in soda pop and pinball machines and used his profits to make his first investment partnership. The rest, as they say, is history.

HOME BUSINESS

As a young man, Lance Schiffman met a Chinese billionaire. In the man's home were original Picassos, Ming vases, and priceless tapestries. Making the most of the opportunity, Lance asked the billionaire how to get rich. The man's advice was simple. "Work the day job," he said. "Get insurance and benefits and stability for your family. You owe them that. But always be looking for the side way to earn. That's where you'll find wealth."

In other words, *win in the margins.*

Lance followed his advice. While he was working nights and graveyard shifts for an airline "winging luggage," as he called it, he tried as many side projects as he could. He owned a triplex, a fast-food restaurant, a gas station, and a florist shop. Some of his ventures were profitable, others not.

One day a friend introduced him to a network marketing company. He signed up and began telling others about the company. They, in turn, told and signed up others. Within two years Lance had more than thirty thousand distributors and was earning well over half a million dollars a year.

More than twelve million Americans are currently involved in network marketing companies. The good news is network marketing can offer low financial risk with a huge potential upside. The bad news is most people do not succeed in making money. I do not believe network marketing is for everyone. For more information about how to select a *legitimate* network marketing opportunity, go to page 90.

A CHRISTMAS GIFT

The most money I've made in my lifetime was on a side project. It wasn't my first such venture. It was my fourteenth.

For me the habit of winning in the margin started when I was young. At the age of twenty, I was working for low wages cleaning up construction sites. Such menial labor gave me ample time to think, though admittedly most of what I thought about was how I could find another job and quit cleaning construction sites.

As I thought over my situation, I realized that there were no vending machines on the job site and that every few hours the construction workers would send someone to a nearby convenience store for soda pop. I saw an opportunity.

That night, on the way home from work, I bought an inexpensive cooler at a secondhand store, then purchased soda pop and candy bars in gross from a nearby price club. The next day I took my cooler to work, selling my products at a dollar each. I doubled my income, making as much on the treats as I did pushing a broom. I eventually accomplished my goal and moved on to another job, but I never stopped trying to win in the margins.

My big hit came ten years later when I decided to self-publish a book I had written as a Christmas present for my daughters. I hadn't intended to publish the book, but after receiving many requests for copies, I decided to print a few. The first year that little book netted me twenty thousand dollars. I reinvested my earnings, and the second year I earned more than four hundred thousand dollars. The third year I earned nearly $4.5 million. That's when I quit my day job.

You could say that I—and the others I've written about here—were just lucky. Of course we were. But as George S. Clason wrote, *"Opportunity is a haughty Goddess who wastes not her time with the unprepared."*

Was it luck that caused me and my colleagues to try again and again to find ways to succeed financially? Was it luck that I noticed a trend with my book? Was it luck that I consulted all the experts I could find about making my book a success? Was it luck that I took copious notes on each marketing venture I tried, evaluating its success and failures? The bottom line is (and you should underline this): *I would never have been lucky had I not been looking for ways to increase my earning ability.*

For free ideas on how to *win in the margins,* visit my Web site today at www.marginswin.com and enter *win* when asked for your passkey.

DOUBLE YOUR WEALTH

While those in the previous examples all hit it big, even earning just a percentage of your regular income each month goes a long way toward building your wealth. As indicated by the table showing compound interest in Lesson Three, if you're earning an average (household) income and are saving 10 percent, you are putting away about $468 a month. If you increase your income by an extra $468 a month and apply it to your nest egg, it is, in the long-term accumulation of wealth, the equivalent of doubling your income.

WEALTH ACCUMULATION AT 10 PERCENT:

Year(s)	Savings
1 Year	**$5,158**
5 Years	**$31,615**
10 Years	**$82,996**
15 Years	**$166,501**
20 Years	**$302,214**
30 Years	**$881,230**
40 Years	**$2,410,579**

WEALTH ACCUMULATION AFTER DOUBLING
YOUR NEST EGG CONTRIBUTION:

Year(s)	Savings
1 Year	**$10,316**
5 Years	**$63,230**
10 Years	**$165,993**
15 Years	**$333,002**
20 Years	**$604,427**
30 Years	**$1,762,459**
40 Years	**$4,821,157**

By increasing your nest egg contribution through earning or saving an additional 10 percent each month, the average household will achieve millionaire status more than seven years earlier. Clearly the path of extra income is worth pursuing. But where do you find the extra income?

As demonstrated by my friend who walked with his head down looking for money, it's all around you. In the Resources section of this book, under *Winning in the Margins with Extra Income,* is a list of possible additional sources of income. However, winning in the margins will come through paying attention to the unique opportunities that already surround you.

I suggested earlier that there's another way to double

your contribution to your nest egg that doesn't include extra earnings. Saving. It's the second way to win in the margins.

WINNING IN THE MARGINS WITH SAVINGS

Money has wings.

—PROVERBS 23:5

Successful wealth builders understand that the world is designed to take their money.

When I was nine years old, my older sister read a book on hypnosis. Then she hypnotized my brother. She told him that he was standing in the middle of the desert beneath a hot, scorching sun and that his feet were glued to the floor. Try as he might, my brother couldn't lift his feet. And even though it was the middle of winter, his skin began to turn red and his forehead beaded with sweat until it dripped down his face. I wouldn't have believed it if I hadn't seen it.

A few years later, as a teenager, I remembered what my sister had done and I began studying how hypnosis worked. Then I began experimenting. I hypnotized many of my friends—even those who didn't believe they could be hypnotized. I was amazed that people with their eyes wide open would see things that weren't there, hear voices, even talk to people who didn't exist. One of my friends, realizing the power of hypnosis, asked if I could create for her an imaginary date with Johnny Depp.

I believe that, to some degree, we are all hypnotized to believe things that aren't true. Essentially, hypnosis is a simple act of suggesting something to the mind. If the hypnotized individual decides to accept the suggestion, then the brain works to make it seem true. Once we have accepted a suggestion, the world around us begins to change to conform to our belief. In other words, *our beliefs shape our reality more than our reality shapes our beliefs.*

Billions of dollars have been spent to suggest to your mind what will make you happy, what you should look like, what you should drive, eat, and wear, and, ultimately, how you should spend your money.

The collective power of those suggestions is likely far more efficacious than you realize. Just look at a thirty-year-old fashion magazine. What were we thinking? Or was someone thinking for us?

Early in my advertising career, I wrote a radio commercial for a local chain of copy centers. In this commercial, I depicted a man talking about the copy centers' new, longer hours with a customer who'd shown up at his store at five minutes past five o'clock needing exactly three thousand copies by morning.

The radio spots ran, and to our surprise, the managers at each of the seven copy centers reported that they had had a rush of people showing up at 5:05 needing exactly three thousand copies by morning.

In the same way that "the Millionaire Mentality" recognizes that the world is designed to take our money, it also knows that the average American has been brainwashed to consume and spend. Billions of dollars are spent in advertising each year to entice you to spend. Market researchers and retail anthropologists specifically study your shopping behavior to more efficiently target you. On the Internet, computers track your spending habits and systematically parade offers in front of you. Politicians and bureaucrats increase fees and taxes. Determined salespeople take courses in learning how to get you to part with your money.

And it's getting worse. Marketers are targeting younger and younger consumers, addicting them to a lifestyle of overconsumption. From 1980 to today, advertising to children in America has increased more than tenfold, from $100 million a year to more than $1 billion.

Successful wealth builders recognize the nature of the real world and therefore carefully scrutinize each expenditure. They learn to win in the margins by keeping more of what they earn.

While most of today's self-help books spout messages

about thinking big, in J. Paul Getty's 1965 book *How to Be Rich,* Getty argued that the problem of financial failure is often attributable to the inability to think small.

The Millionaire Mentality, he wrote "gives meticulous attention to even the smallest details and misses no opportunities to reduce costs in his own or his employer's business."

This "Millionaire Mentality" can be applied to all aspects of financial endeavor, from business to personal spending. There are four key mind-sets that characterize the wealth builder:

1. The Millionaire Mentality carefully considers each expenditure.
2. The Millionaire Mentality believes that freedom and power are better than momentary pleasure.
3. The Millionaire Mentality does not equate spending with happiness.
4. The Millionaire Mentality protects the nest egg.

The Millionaire Mentality Carefully Considers Each Expenditure

There are three questions that the successful wealth builder asks himself before he spends his money.

1. Is this expenditure really necessary? (Or is it possible to get the same personal effect without using money or using less of it?)

One of the best-dressed women I know is a single mother living on a very limited income. "How can you afford such a beautiful wardrobe?" I asked her. She smiled and said it was her secret. Later on she offered to tell me. "I only buy used clothing—high quality—but preowned by some rich person. I let them lose the value." Same effect, without the financial effect.

A few years ago I was in Venice, standing near the gondolas by the Piazza San Marco waiting for the rest of my group to arrive. I had lived in Italy for more than a year and spoke enough Italian to be conversant. The gondoliers, however, assumed that I was just another American tourist, so they didn't worry about what they said in front of me.

"How much do I charge this group?" one of the gondoliers asked.

"Fifty dollars for Japanese. Forty dollars for Americans. Twenty dollars for Italians."

"How do you determine what to charge?" I asked the man in Italian.

Embarrassed that I had understood him, he finally answered, "Whatever they will pay."

Most prices are determined in this very way, and as such are usually far more negotiable than you think. This doesn't mean you have to become a hardened haggler. Simple, soft-voiced inquiry is often just as effective—if not more so. Recently I was shopping for some computer equipment at a local electronics dealer. After the salesperson had demonstrated the equipment and quoted a price, I simply asked him if they matched the lowest price available. "I hate buying something and the next day finding it cheaper somewhere else," I explained. He thought about it, then said, "Just a minute." He pulled up a comparison site on the In-

56

ternet, and we immediately found the same equipment available for $140 less.

"There's the price," I said.

He not only sold it to me for that price, but threw in a few other complimentary items as well.

SEVEN GOLDEN WORDS

A salesman friend of mine was trying to negotiate a deal with a large client. But when he quoted his client his bid, the man's forehead creased with concern. "Is that the best you can do?" he asked.

My friend began to squirm. He left the room and called his boss. "We've got to do better," he said. His boss gave him a better price. Newly confident with his bid, my friend sat back down with his client. "We can go 3 percent less."

The man still looked concerned. "Is that *really* the best you can do?"

My friend, more certain that he was about to lose the account, went back to the phone. He again talked to his boss, who conceded one more percent discount. Afraid that it wasn't going to be enough, my friend threw in a portion of his own sales commission. Still, the client didn't seem impressed. "Is that truly the best you can do?"

My friend sighed. "I'm sorry," he said, "but it is."

The man smiled. "Fine. I'll sign the order. I was just making sure that it really was your best offer."

Only then did my friend realize that the man would have paid the first price quoted.

Just seven simple words: is that the best you can do. Of all the advice in this book, the seven golden words are likely to provide you the most immediate and surprising success. A friend of mine who was in the middle of building a home claimed to have saved more than $25,000 by using the seven golden words. Another reader reported saving more than a thousand dollars within two hours of learning the seven golden words. We hear these success stories regularly. Not that this surprises me. I have a rather large and growing collection of my own. The seven golden words work.

Winning in the margins means pushing the limit to see just how low you can purchase—especially on the big-ticket items.

A financial consultant once said to me, "It drives me crazy the way people compartmentalize their money. They'll clip coupons to save thirty-five cents on a can of soup, then throw thousands away on a big purchase because they didn't bother to compare prices or even ask if they could get it for less."

I once saved a third of the price of a car just by checking the Internet and comparing prices. I found a rare car I liked at a dealership. After inquiring about the price, I immediately went home and searched the Internet. I found the identical car for much less in a different state.

I went back to the dealership and made an offer for 30 percent less than the quoted price. At first the salesman laughed. Then I showed him a printout of the car in California and told him I could fly my whole family to Disneyland for a week, then drive the car back myself and still save more than ten thousand dollars. I asked him what he would do. He called back the next day to accept my offer.

LESS IS MORE

As long as we're asking the question, "Is this expenditure really necessary?" something should be written about consumption. Americans currently overconsume at record (and embarrassing) levels. The quest to have more can be seen in our homes as well as our waistlines. In 1950, the average home was 1,100 square feet. In 1970, it had increased to 1,400 square feet. By the year 2000, the average home was more than 2,000 square feet, despite the fact that families have gotten smaller.

As a nation we are spending more and more and enjoying it less. Peculiarly, more people surveyed in the fifties described themselves as "rich" than do today.

Curtailing the pattern of overconsumption is an important step not just in saving, but in freeing ourselves from our possessions. Psychologically, in spite of all we've been told (or sold), more is less and less is more. This is corroborated by a study that showed that 86 percent of Americans felt happier after having voluntarily cut back on consumption.

2. Is this expenditure contributing to my wealth or taking from it?

Of course not all expenditures can be assets, but continually asking this question helps wealth builders redirect the use of their money. It's no coincidence that the wealthy put their money in their homes instead of their cars. Homes usually *appreciate.* Cars almost always *depreciate.*

3. Is this an impulse purchase or a planned purchase? Am I being pressured to make an expenditure I'm not certain about?

Candy bars and magazines line the checkout stands like thugs, waiting to jump you as you pull out your wallet or purse. Late-night infomercials come at you when you're tired and your resistance is down.

The impulse buy is the mainstay of the American retail establishment. The layout of the grocery store testifies to this, which is why the essentials—meat, eggs, and milk—are always at the back of the store, making you pass aisle after aisle of possible impulse purchases. And it works. Most grocery stores estimate that more than 50 percent of purchases are impulse purchases.

You've heard the adage "Never shop with an empty stomach." This wisdom should be applied whenever money is concerned. Buy what you mean to buy. Whether it's for groceries or a new car, save time and money by shopping with a list.

GOING ONCE, GOING TWICE . . .

Early in our marriage, we made a commitment to never make any large purchase "on impulse." If the salesperson said he needed an answer "right now," then the answer was "no." In twenty years, we haven't once regretted walking away from a strong-arm sales pitch. Not once. In fact, whenever we found ourselves being pressured by an aggressive salesperson—one who was insisting that we had to buy now or let a once-in-a-lifetime opportunity pass—it was very empowering to be able to say no.

The funny thing is that despite all the threats that the

opportunity would pass, it never did. Not once that I can remember. But many times *we* passed. Often, after a good night's sleep, we decided we really could live without an automatic sock stacker after all.

Unfortunately, on one occasion I broke the rule. Against my wife's counsel, I bought under pressure. I fell in love with a piece of property. It was heaven on earth, I thought, and I was afraid that if I delayed I would lose it. I enjoyed my decision for three months, rationalized it for another six months, and regretted it for six long, painful years. That's how long it took me to get out from under the debt after losing hundreds of thousands of dollars.

Again, this program is not about deprivation. It's about not wasting money. Buy whatever you want, if you have the money. Just make sure that you really want it and will enjoy it for at least as long as you have to pay for it.

REALIZE YOUR SAVINGS

Whenever you save money from using one of these techniques, it is important that you realize those savings by moving the money saved into your nest egg. For instance, a friend of mine was about to pay off a hospital bill and had already written out the check when he decided to try the seven golden words. The hospital, apologetically, told him that it could only discount the bill by 10 percent. He was delighted, of course. He tore up the check he had written and wrote two more—one for the revised hospital bill and the second to his nest egg for the 10 percent he had just saved.

Remember, if you are able to to save just $100 a month and you faithfully transfer it to your nest egg, in forty years (compounded at the average S&P 500 rate of 10.2 percent) that little extra saving will be worth close to $700,000!

The Millionaire Mentality Believes That Freedom and Power Are Better Than Momentary Pleasure

Too many people spend money they haven't earned, to buy things they don't want, to impress people they don't like.

— WILL SMITH

The sirens of credit are luring Americans to the rocks of disaster. Their enticing song, "Buy now, *pay* later," is indeed truth in advertising, though it was certainly not intended to be. *Pay* is exactly what America is doing. The price we pay to have it now is quite clear: broken marriages, homes, health, and lives. The successful wealth builder understands the danger of debt and knows that the primary way to avoid it is by delaying gratification.

A decade ago, *Time* magazine reported that brain research suggests that emotions, not IQ, may be the true measure of human intelligence. And the ability to delay gratification is one of the key indicators of emotional intelligence. Interestingly, it is also an indicator of future success.

THE MARSHMALLOW EXPERIMENT

A group of scientists created an experiment to test emotional intelligence. They told four-year-old children that they could have one marshmallow now or, if they could wait while the researchers ran an errand, they could have two. They then placed marshmallows in front of the children and left the room. Some of the children waited for the second marshmallow, while others immediately devoured the one in front of them. The follow-up research was most fascinating.

Those children who could delay gratification "generally grew up to be better adjusted, more popular, adventurous, confident and dependable. Those who couldn't were more likely to be lonely, easily frustrated and stubborn. They buckled under stress and shied away from challenges."

In addition, those who could delay gratification also scored an average of 210 points higher on the SATs.

MY FATHER'S EPIPHANY

I'll never forget the night my father called us together for a special family meeting. It was after we had lost our home, and all of us children had gathered in the living room of our little duplex. The mood in our home that night was as somber as a funeral, and my father looked distraught. We didn't know why he had brought us together, but from his countenance, we knew it couldn't be good.

He looked us over sadly, then said: "I've spent the last three days figuring out why, after all these years of hard work, I have nothing to show for it but bills. Do you know where it all goes?"

"To us?" one of us asked.

"No," he said grimly, "I wish. It goes to interest. All those heartbeats went to paying interest to make someone else wealthy. Delay gratification. Never borrow money."

Earlier, in the Third Lesson, I demonstrated the power of compound interest. Never forget that compound interest is just as powerful working against you as it is working for you. What might seem like a small expense now can, in the long run, steal your wealth. Simply put, there are two kinds of people: those who earn interest and those who pay it. That's the fundamental difference between the wealthy and the desperate. The Millionaire Mentality sees clearly the danger of credit and knows that freedom and power are infinitely better than short-lived pleasure.

BUT I DESERVE IT . . .

An employee of mine desired a new car. It was too expensive for their income, but she was intent on convincing me that it was the right choice for her.

"My husband is about to get a raise. Why shouldn't we have a nice car? Don't we deserve it?"

Deserve it? She had just regurgitated the greatest marketing sham ever propagated on the American consumer— the result of years of advertising brainwashing. She deserves what? To find happiness based on something that will decay and lose value within a year, yet will continue to financially enslave her long after her infatuation with the metal is gone? In the words of my teenage daughter: Is this a good thing?

After several discussions, she reluctantly chose not to buy the car. A year later we revisited her decision.

"I'm so glad I didn't buy that car," she said. "It doesn't even interest me anymore. And my husband didn't get the raise we had planned on. Had we bought that car, we would have found ourselves deep in debt and struggling just to make payments."

The next time you hear someone say, "You deserve it," red flags should instantly go up in your mind. Someone is trying to take your wealth. Someone is trying to steal your dreams for themselves. What you really deserve is peace of mind, individual freedom, and personal power.

THEM VS. US

With so much wealth at stake, it's no wonder banks and retail businesses work so hard to extend you interest. And their efforts are paying off. In 1970, only 17 percent of American households had a bank-issued credit card. By 2001, that number had increased to 73 percent. Today Americans own more than one billion credit cards. I met a woman at one of my seminars who had twenty-seven different credit cards.

In addition to the practice of companies offering special incentives to entice you to take their charge cards, there are other credit-inducing tactics you might not have considered.

A typical sales tactic is the no-pain add-on purchase. You've likely been victimized by it.

As a teenager I worked at a fast-food restaurant. Whenever we took an order, we were required to ask customers if they wanted fries or a drink to go with their order. Initially, my thought was: If they wanted fries or a drink, they would have asked for it. Not so. More than half the people I asked changed their order. This technique works on larger purchases as well, from cars to houses. Unfortunately, outside the fast-food world, there is interest involved.

"Would you like a refrigerator to go with that house?"

You've just come to the end of the long and tedious process of qualifying for a home loan. Before the last signature is inked, you are asked, "Do you need any appliances? We could easily add a few luxuries onto that loan. How about a refrigerator?"

What most home buyers don't consider is that this additional purchase goes right on the end of their thirty-year mortgage. Even at a low interest rate like 5 percent, after five years the average cost for a $1,000 refrigerator is nearly double the sales price. And Americans wonder where their money goes.

WHAT KIND OF FOOL?

The poor and the uneducated are particularly susceptible to interest schemes. That's one of the reasons they stay poor. Back when I worked at an advertising agency, we had a client who rented out electronic appliances. You've likely seen similar television commercials: Come to Shams-Rent-to-Own, where you can have it today!

As I was listing the weekly price of a VCR for a television commercial, something didn't look right. I called the store manager.

"This price couldn't be right," I said. "It says $19.99 a week for this VCR."

"No, that's right."

"Twenty dollars a week? For how long?"

"A year."

"You're kidding me. That adds up to more than a thousand dollars for this VCR. It couldn't have cost more than a hundred dollars."

"Actually, we got it for only sixty."

"What kind of fool would pay more than a thousand dollars for a sixty-dollar VCR?" I asked.

"People who want it now."

• • •

Successful nest eggers are emotionally intelligent. They can wait—even when it's not the easiest course of action. Because of my belief in the Five Lessons, my wife and I decided before we were married that we would never go in debt. We found the engagement ring and the diamond we wanted, but I didn't have enough money to pay for it.

Believe me, I was sorely tempted to break my rule and go into debt. I had other pressures besides the jeweler. To start, a beautiful fiancée whom I wanted to impress—not to mention a future father-in-law who was certain that I was going to keep his daughter barefoot and pregnant. But with my fiancée's support, we held fast to the rule. We put down what money we had to hold the diamond, then had a cubic zirconium set into the ring until we could pay cash for the real stone. No one knew the difference except us. A few months later, I paid off the diamond and we swapped the stones.

For the successful nest egger, freedom and power are infinitely better than momentary satisfaction.

The Millionaire Mentality Does Not Equate Spending with Happiness

Money is not required to buy one necessity of the soul.

— HENRY DAVID THOREAU

Too many of us have adopted shopping as catharsis. "Shopping is therapy," says a television commercial. "Money can buy happiness—just don't pay retail." Equating spending with happiness is the first step to financial self-destruction. Recently, I met a woman whose daughter was working three jobs trying to keep up with her $50,000 credit card debt.

"What did she spend all that money on?" I asked.

"Stuff. Clothes and stuff. She had a bad marriage and

she's just trying to fill the void. Unfortunately, all she does now is work."

The successful nest egger fosters gratitude as a strategy against materialism and unhappiness.

One of the great antidotes for *consumption as therapy* is found in the character trait of gratitude. And the Millionaire Mentality knows this. We live in a world of abundance. The things that bring the greatest joy are not reserved for the wealthy alone. The simplest of pleasures can bring the greatest happiness. What price can we put on inner peace? Or health? Or friendship or love?

Those who forget to be grateful for what they have often waste their lives and wealth looking for more. Their thirst becomes unquenchable as they seek to buy what cannot be bought. It doesn't matter if these people have one dollar or a billion, because they will never have contentment or happiness. They may be in a high tax bracket, but they will never be truly wealthy.

The Millionaire Mentality Protects the Nest Egg

There was a time when a fool and his money were soon parted, but now it happens to everybody.

— ADLAI E. STEVENSON

Successful nest eggers do not risk what they cannot afford to lose. This applies to both investing and living. High-risk, get-rich-quick schemes and other forms of gambling do not appeal to them.

Additionally, successful wealth builders purchase proper insurance to protect their growing wealth.

A study conducted by a Harvard University Law School professor found that medical bills and other financial effects of illness or injury contributed to nearly half of the more than one million personal bankruptcy filings in the United States. Having proper insurance can make the difference between financial peace of mind and catastrophe.

Is the person I'm trusting with my wealth sufficiently skilled to handle my money?

In *The Richest Man in Babylon,* George S. Clason tells the story of a man who entrusts his hard-earned money to his friend, a bricklayer, to purchase precious gems. Of course, the bricklayer knows nothing about precious gems, and he returns with worthless pieces of glass. "Trust bricklayers with advice about bricks," says his mentor.

Be especially careful with your money when it comes to family. This is what I call the Brother-in-law Syndrome.

As your wealth grows, you will be set upon by others (usually in-laws, it seems) to fund their schemes and business ventures. They will often use emotional manipulation to get you to part with your money. Be kind and simply say, "Let's take your plan to an expert in the field." In most cases, this will end the inquiry. It's not easy to say no to a loved one. But seeing them lose your money is worse. Much worse. And in the end no one is happy.

●　　●　　●

Whether you win in the margins through creating extra income or through savings, both will get you to where you want to be. But serious wealth accumulators employ both to help them reach their goals.

LESSON FOUR

Win in the Margins

LESSON FIVE

Give Back

> All you have shall some day be given;
> therefore give now, that the season of
> giving may be yours and not your
> inheritors'.
>
> —KAHLIL GIBRAN

The great philanthropist Andrew Carnegie said, "The problem of our age is the proper administration of wealth." To Carnegie, there were only three possible means by which a man of great wealth could dispose of his fortune: (1) he could leave it to his family; (2) he could bequeath it in his will for public purposes; (3) he could share it during his lifetime for the public benefit.

Of the first he said, "The thoughtful man must shortly say, 'I would as soon leave to my son a curse as the almighty dollar.'" History is replete with cautionary tales bearing out his words.

Carnegie found the second option equally objectionable,

as heirs would likely contest any substantial will, thereby leaving a legacy of greed, contention, and bitterness in the wake of the benefactor's death.

Only the third option, the sharing of money in his lifetime, could he accept. Said Carnegie, "This, then, is held to be the duty of the man of wealth: To set an example of modest, unostentatious living, shunning display or extravagance; to provide moderately for the legitimate wants of those dependent upon him; and, after doing so, to consider all surplus revenues which come to him simply as trust funds which he is called upon to administer."

FRIEND OR FOE?

Ultimately, the most honorable and enjoyable use of money is in serving others. Freely giving of our wealth is also the only way to fully protect ourselves from our wealth. Yes, money is a powerful ally. But it can also be a spiritual and emotional enemy. If money becomes what you live for, you will eventually conclude that life is not worth living.

While money is an inescapable part of life, it's not life. Hoarding wealth will make your life small and cold. Giving will warm and expand it. As Eleanor Roosevelt said, "When you cease [to give], you begin to die."

LIFE'S BALANCE SHEET

A few years back, I took my oldest daughter, Jenna, on a daddy-daughter date to the Amazon jungles of Peru on a humanitarian mission. I wanted her to not only realize how much we have to be grateful for, but to learn to serve others who are less fortunate.

Our journey turned into an extraordinary adventure. We hiked deep into the jungle with machetes, and at one point we ran out of food. The only meat we had was piranha. (It tastes like chicken.) We set up a clinic in the small jungle town of Puerto Maldonada, and the Quechuan natives came from miles around.

Almost two weeks later, at the end of our excursion, Jenna and I were in the Lima, Peru, airport when I asked her what she had learned from the experience.

"Let me think about it," she said.

Twelve hours later we were in Chicago's O'Hare International Airport waiting for our connection, and I noticed that Jenna was crying. When I asked her what was wrong, she replied, "Dad, we have so much and they have so little." She looked down for a moment, then added, "I know what I've learned. We love those whom we serve."

Success in life cannot be measured on a balance sheet. I believe that the truest measure of achievement is the degree to which we've learned to love. And service, through sharing our wealth and our time, is love made visible.

FINANCIAL KARMA

While generosity feeds the soul, ironically it also feeds the pocketbook. I believe that we receive as we give. It is written in the Bible:

> Will a man rob God? Yet ye have robbed me. But ye say, Wherein have we robbed thee? In tithes and offerings. . . . Prove me now herewith . . . if I will not open you the windows of heaven, and pour you out a blessing, that there shall not be room enough to receive it."
>
> —Malachi 2:8–10

While I don't believe that this promise written in the Bible applies solely to financial blessings, I believe there are karmic principles attached to wealth. We get back when we give. As such, it's important to give not just after we've achieved wealth, but as part of the process.

I have tithed 10 percent of my income since I was eight years old, and in spite of the hardships my family has sometimes faced, I have never felt the loss of this money. Rather, I have felt specifically blessed for my contributions.

On one occasion when my business was doing poorly, I called my accountant and asked him to review my financial records over the last year to see if I had, in fact, paid a true tithe of 10 percent. He called back the next day and told me that I was $800 short. I wrote a check immediately and sent it off. The next day I had three calls from former clients needing work done immediately. Coincidence? Maybe. But I don't think so. I've heard similar stories from friends and associates of different faiths around the world.

The sin of the desert is knowing where the water is and not telling anyone.

In addition to sharing your wealth, you have a responsibility to share the lessons of proper money management with others. Within twenty-four hours of reading this book, teach these Five Lessons to a spouse, a teenage son or daughter, or a friend. In the next week share this book with those you care about. As you share these principles, you will see firsthand the gift of giving back. Teaching the Five Lessons to others will help you internalize them and become better prepared to live and enjoy the fruits of them yourself.

CONCLUSION

Is It Ever Too Late to Start?

A few months ago, a reporter was in my office interviewing me about one of my charities when he noticed the cover of *The Five Lessons* on my desk. He asked me what the book was about. I briefly explained the five principles of wealth, then invited him to attend one of my seminars.

"I could use that," he said, "but I'm afraid it's too late." To my surprise, his eyes watered. "My daughter called this morning. She needs money for college. I had to tell her that I can't help her. I just don't have it."

Is it ever too late to live these principles? My answer is a resounding "No." Yes, it can be too late to take full advantage of the power of compound interest, but progress is progress. It's never too late to do the right thing or the smart thing and enjoy the benefits it brings.

Hearkening back to my earlier example of Heather and James: even if they never reach their goal of complete financial freedom (although I believe that they will), they are already light-years ahead of where they were, and are free of their daily hurt and the bondage of debt. They are already enjoying more of the blessings of living in this free and abundant country. Most importantly, they have hope. And hope is always worth striving for.

IN THE END

We end where we began. Life is not about money. It's about God. It's about love. It's about family and relationships. In sharing with you these principles, it is my hope that you will always give back, that you might find life's true abundance.

All millionaires die, but there are no dead millionaires. Their wealth passes on. As Ray Kroc, the founder of Mc-Donald's, was fond of saying, "I've never seen a Brinks truck following a hearse."

If you have lived successfully, your estate will consist of more than material possessions, and your legacy will be more than cash, stocks, and IRAs. Remember this, that you may use your wealth wisely, find true abundance, and live, as Mark Twain said, "so that even the undertaker mourns your passing."

In the end, this is true wealth.

LESSON ONE

Decide to Be Wealthy

LESSON TWO

Take Responsibility for Your Money

LESSON THREE

Keep a Portion of Everything You Earn

LESSON FOUR

Win in the Margins

LESSON FIVE

Give Back

THE FIVE LESSONS

Resources

WINNING IN THE MARGINS
WITH EXTRA INCOME

Remember, winning in the margins with extra income will come through paying attention to the unique opportunities that already surround you.

JOBS TO INCREASE YOUR INCOME

- Wait tables on the weekends.
- Turn your hobbies into jobs.
- Learn to make jewelry and sell it at local fairs.
- Teach cooking classes.
- Referee.
- Teach piano lessons.
- Babysit.
- House-sit.
- Clean houses or office buildings.
- Refurbish furniture and sell it to consignment stores.
- Pick up a paper route.
- Repair cars.
- Put up and take down other peoples' Christmas lights.
- Do freelance work.
- Start a lawn-care business.
- Donate plasma.
- Help coach a local sporting team.
- Become a massage therapist.
- Teach private swim lessons.
- Sell homemade rolls or treats around the holidays.

- Sell gift baskets.
- Get certified and teach aerobics or water aerobics.
- If you are good at photography, start a small business.

- Breed animals.
- Teach language lessons.
- Look into credible multilevel marketing opportunities.

HOW TO SELECT A LEGITIMATE NETWORK MARKETING COMPANY

Before starting any business, ask yourself these questions. 1. Do you *really* like the product or service and is it *reasonably* priced? 2. If it's a health-related product, are the product's claims substantiated by the FDA? 3. Is it inexpensive to join? (A start-up fee of more than $100 is an indication of a possible scam.) 4. Can you comfortably afford the monthly product cost and would you use the product even if you didn't hope to profit from it? 5. Are you willing to maximize the tax advantages of a home business? 6. Are you willing to work hard and are there people willing to support you?

If you can answer yes to all six questions, network marketing might be a means for you to win in the margins. Before joining, read everything you can about a company, including reports from the FTC.

For a free online report on how you can increase your earning ability, visit my Web site at www.marginswin.com and enter *win* when asked for your passkey.

WINNING IN THE MARGINS
WITH SAVINGS

When winning in the margins with savings, always remember to apply the four mind-sets.

1. The Millionaire Mentality carefully considers each expenditure.
2. The Millionaire Mentality believes that freedom and power are better than momentary pleasure.
3. The Millionaire Mentality does not equate spending with happiness.
4. The Millionaire Mentality protects the nest egg.

As you fill out your monthly Cash Flow form, review each expenditure, then begin looking for ways to save. Remember that the Internet has put more power in consumers' hands than ever before. Be sure to take full advantage of it. In each applicable category we have included a list of Web sites to help you save.

Don't expect all of the suggestions to be right for you. Check off the ones that you find helpful. Remember: the goal is to reduce your expenditures by an additional 10 percent of your income so as to double your contribution to your nest egg.

BUILDING THE NEST EGG

- Put a minimum of 10 percent of your monthly salary and 90–100 percent of extra income into your nest egg.
- If you receive a pay increase, put the extra away in savings.
- Take advantage of banks' and brokerage firms' automatic-withdrawal plans that will take money from your checking account and put it into your savings account.
- When you have finished paying off your debt, divert the money you were using to pay it off into your nest egg.
- Collect all your spare change in a jar; when it is full, deposit it into your nest egg. It will add up to more than you think. In our research, a cup of miscellaneous coins is worth about $24.

MORTGAGE AND RENT

- You can save thousands of dollars in interest charges by shopping for the lowest rate. Always obtain more than one quote before accepting a loan. Be sure to ask about all fees involved.

- Use an adjustable rate mortgage (ARM) only if you can't afford a fixed rate loan or if you intend to sell the home within a few years.
- Choose the shortest-term loan you can afford.
- Be cautious in taking out home equity loans. The loans reduce or may even eliminate the equity that you have built up in your home. (Equity is the cash you would have if you sold your house and paid off your mortgage loans.)
- By making just one extra mortgage payment every year you can reduce the time span of the loan by up to seven years. Plan, right now, to double your payment one month this year or split the amount of thirteen payments into twelve even payments.
- Check the tax assessment of your property. If you think you are paying taxes based on too high an evaluation, contact the assessor's office and file an appeal. According to the Association of Assessing Offices, *over half* of all appeals result in the reduction of taxes.
- Look into refinancing your mortgage anytime rates falls a half percentage below your existing rate.
- Drop private mortgage insurance (PMI) if it is no longer necessary. While this insurance is sometimes required when you first purchase a home, in most cases it can be

dropped after you have paid off 20 percent of the loan. Ask your lender about termination rules. It may have been done automatically, but if not you could save an extra $25 a month.

- Rent out a room or basement.
- Find a roommate.
- Rent from a private party rather than a corporation when possible—you may avoid automatic periodic increases in rent.
- Spend no more than 25 percent of your monthly gross income on your rent. The extra money you allocate for rent in a slightly more upscale complex means less money for your other expenses: utilities, loan payments, entertainment, food, and, most important, savings.

FOOD

- Shop with a list. Plan your shopping based on sales and specials and avoid impulse purchasing.
- Comparison shop by looking at the unit price listed on the shelf below each item. The unit price indicates the cost per pound or ounce.
- Join a wholesale superstore such as Costco or Sam's Club; buy necessities such as some food staples and toiletries in bulk.

- Eat out more frugally, and avoid beverages; many restaurants make a large profit on beverages, especially alcohol. Few people check the price of drinks, and restaurateurs know this. On one occasion I found that a simple soda cost nearly as much as some of a particular restaurant's entrées.
- Ordering vegetarian meals saves money, as they generally cost less than meat-based entrées.
- Try brown-bagging it twice a week instead of eating out. Some consumer groups estimate that this will save you at least $500 per year. (Not to mention the calories.)
- Do your grocery shopping on double coupon days.
- Purchase generic brands. According to some experts, this can save you an average of 40 percent off your annual grocery bill.
- Watch for discounts on nonperishables that you buy regularly and stock up when they are on sale.
- Shop for meat early or late in the day, when certain cuts may be at a discount.
- Prepackaged goods cost more. Cook from scratch more often.
- Always keep the ingredients for at least one quick-and-easy meal in the house to avoid unplanned eating out when tired or in a hurry.
- Always check receipts for accuracy, especially with coupons and produce.

- Check prices on grocery store sales. Actual savings may be insignificant or misleading.
- Buy loss leaders. These are the items on the front page of the ad and are often sold at cost just to get you into the store.
- Fresh-food areas usually have a section featuring items that will expire within a few days. These items can be discounted anywhere from 50 to 70 percent.
- Avoid purchasing nongrocery products, such as cosmetics and household items, in grocery stores. These products are usually marked up 25 percent higher than they are in discount drugstores.
- Grow your own garden.
- Search the Internet for freebies and coupons from manufacturers. (See list at the end of this section.)
- Have a potluck or barbecue dinner with friends instead of going out to dinner.
- You've heard it before: Never shop hungry. Researchers have shown that, on the average, consumers spend 10 percent more when they go to the grocery store hungry.
- Carry a calculator with you whenever you shop.
- Do your grocery shopping on Monday. Prices on average are lower.
- The best all-purpose cleaner is chlorine bleach. You can clean toilets, sinks, floors, and walls and potentially save $20 a month.

FOOD SAVINGS WEB SITES:

- coupons.com
- q-pon.com
- hotcoupons.com
- coolsavings.com
- couponcart.com
- couponorganizer.com
- frugalshopper.com
- valpak.com

UTILITIES

- Check windows and doors for air leaks. Use caulk to seal them. A package of caulk will cost less than $5. Check your local home-improvement stores for more ideas.
- Insulate your water heater. Although your water heater and pipes may be insulated on the inside, they can lose heat and energy through the outside casing. Insulating blankets are available at most home-improvement stores. They are easy to install and can save you up to 3 percent on monthly heating bills.
- Turn down your heat by five degrees and wear a sweater. This could save 15 percent on your heating bills. During the summer months, use the air conditioner as little as

possible. You will see dramatic savings in your electric bill.

- Contact your energy supplier. Your local electric and gas companies may have various reduced-rate plans depending on your age, income level, or dwelling.
- Replace 100-watt bulbs with 60-watt bulbs.
- Sometimes the best way to save money takes money. Replacing old appliances with newer and more energy efficient ones may save you money in the long run.
- Install a water-flow regulator in showerheads and toilet bowls. This can reduce the amount of water use by 50 percent without a noticeable difference in pressure.
- Buy energy-saving light bulbs.
- Unplug appliances.
- Fix leaky faucets. Leaky faucets can waste six to ten gallons of water per day.
- Install dimmers in living areas such as dining rooms and bedrooms. Lights dimmed 15 percent reduce energy consumption by 15 percent.
- Use electric timers to conserve energy. (These can be purchased at any home-improvement store.)
- Use a programmable thermostat to lower the heat at night after you're asleep. Also, lower your heat when you're not home.
- Pay for a year's worth of cable or satellite television or

Internet. This may help you avoid extra monthly charges.

- Use high-energy appliances such as dishwashers and washing machines on off-peak hours. (Call your utility company to find out about different rates for on- and off-peak times.)
- Close heat vents in any room that does not need to be heated.
- Attics should be insulated to avoid heat or air conditioning from escaping.
- Double-pane your windows.
- As mentioned earlier, renting to own is likely the most expensive way to purchase something (such as a VCR). If you can't wait, find another way to finance the item you want to buy.
- Be aware of your phone usage. Calls made after 5 P.M. are cheaper in most places than calls placed between 8 A.M. and 5 P.M.
- Shop around for a calling plan that best fits your needs.
- Turn off lights, television, and other appliances when leaving a room.
- Learn to fix minor things around the house to avoid having to pay a plumber or handyman.
- Check your utility bill. One study showed that four out of five companies overcharged on their utilities. Utili-

ties' auditing companies report that on the average most homeowners are overcharged by 20 percent.

TRANSPORTATION: CAR PAYMENTS AND EXPENSES

- When buying a new car, check out new car guides to help you with model information and pricing.
- Don't buy more car (or cars) than you need. Most of my millionaire friends drive economy cars.
- Before you buy a used car, compare the seller's asking price with the average retail price in a blue book. Try www.kellybluebook.com.
- Have a mechanic you trust inspect the car before you agree to purchase.
- Always think long-term when buying a car. You pay much more than the initial cost of the car, including gas, insurance, registration fees, maintenance, and repairs.
- Buy regular unleaded gas. Many studies have shown that more expensive fuel isn't worth it. (Check with your dealer or mechanic.)
- Fill up on gas when shopping at a warehouse wholesaler where gas is cheaper.
- Carpooling with coworkers twice a week could save you up to $20 a month.

- Buy commuter passes where available.
- Don't use credit cards to buy gas if it requires paying a higher price.
- Service cars regularly, before problems develop. Change the oil in your car (yourself) every 3,000 miles. Keep wheels aligned and balanced.
- If a mechanic finds a problem during routine maintenance, get a second opinion and another estimate before making repairs.
- Don't buy tires that are said to last thousands of miles longer than you intend to drive your car. It is a lot more expensive and unnecessary.
- By paying cash, you can save a nickel per gallon at many gas pumps.
- Use air-conditioning in your car only when needed. The extra load on the engine severely reduces mileage.
- Avoid poor driving habits. Maintaining a constant speed over a long distance saves gas. Excess braking wastes fuel up to 20 percent.
- An interesting Web site to check local gas prices is: gasbuddy.com.
- A friend of mine figured out a way to drive cars for free. In fact, he actually made money on them. Every six months or so he'd go to local car auctions and buy a car. He'd drive the car for six months, then turn around and

sell it at a profit. He'd then go back to the auction and start the process all over again.

AIR TRAVEL

- Fly on Sundays rather than Saturdays.
- Book flights early; most flights increase in cost when you book less than two weeks in advance.
- Be flexible when booking flights.
- Buy tickets during the week. Oftentimes fares are raised temporarily for the weekend.
- Ask about discounts for seniors and children.
- Be sure to check on discount carriers.

WEB SITES FOR HOTEL, TRAVEL, AND AIRFARE DISCOUNTS

- expedia.com
- hotels.com
- cheapfares.com
- 11thhourvacation.com
- hotwire.com
- havekids-willtravel.com. This site offers a fascinating guide to family travel anywhere in the world at remarkably reduced rates—oftentimes free.

AUTOMOBILE INSURANCE

- Always shop around to get the best possible insurance rates. A study by Progressive Insurance shows that the cost of an auto insurance policy for the same driver with the same or comparable coverage can vary from company to company by as much as $1,000 a year.
- Raise your deductible. According to the Insurance Information Institute, raising your deductible from $200 to $500 could reduce your collision and comprehensible cost 15 to 30 percent.
- Make sure your current policy accurately reflects your needs. It is important to update your information on your driving record, age, and the model of car you drive. The correct information can reduce your rate.
- You may receive added discounts by holding a policy with one company for a long period of time.

MEDICAL INSURANCE

- As explained in Lesson Four, always have at least minimal medical coverage to protect yourself and your nest egg against catastrophe.
- Always get second opinions before making major medical decisions.

- If you spend time in a hospital, carefully check the itemized bill to be sure that there were no incorrect charges. One consumer-advocacy group reports that 90 percent of hospital bills contain errors, with overcharges accounting for approximately two-thirds of those errors.
- Buy generic drugs and no-frills vitamins. You can save up to 50 percent on some drugs. (Always check with your doctor before taking generic drugs.) Shop around for prescriptions on the Internet or use a mail-order company. The average savings are 30 percent.

HOME OWNER'S INSURANCE

- Make your home more resistant to disaster. (Find out how through your insurance agent or a company representative.)
- When deciding how much insurance to buy, don't include the value of the land under your home, as it isn't at risk for theft or fire.
- Install smoke detectors, dead-bolt locks, or burglar alarms to cut your premiums. (Ask your insurance agent if you qualify for any discounts.)
- Review the value of your possessions yearly to be sure you're paying only for coverage you need. (These should already be on your Net Worth form)
- If you are paying home owner's insurance through the

government, look into private insurance, as it may be cheaper.

DEBT PAYMENTS

- Use credit cards that don't charge an annual fee, such as Discover, GM, Ford, AFBA Industrial Bank, or USAA federal savings.
- Refinance your mortgage for a lower interest rate and use that money to pay off existing debt.
- Keep the two credit cards with the lowest interest rates.
- When paying monthly credit card bills, pay the full amount or calculate how much you can afford to pay over the minimum.
- When applicable (see Lesson Three) use some of your savings to get out of debt.
- Seek help through a nonprofit consumer credit counseling service, or seek out a financial support group.
- Resolve that you will use your credit cards only for essentials over the next six months.

CLOTHING

- Shop clearance sales. (When stores begin to put out next season's clothes you can save 30 to 75 percent on your family's clothing budget.)

- Avoid clothes that must be dry-cleaned. Buy machine-washable clothes rather than silks or wools.
- Hand-wash and iron your shirts instead of dry-cleaning them.
- Shop at thrift stores or upscale clothing consignment stores.
- Shop for children's school clothes after school starts to avoid the rush and peak prices.
- Minimize accessories that won't be used frequently.
- Stick with classic styles and don't always change your wardrobe to suit current fashion trends.
- Shop for only a few hours at a time—you'll be less likely to buy impulsively.

CLOTHING AND HOME ACCESSORIES WEB SITES

- bluefly.com
- overstock.com
- jumpondeals.com
- justdeals.com
- gogoshoppers.com
- smartbargains.com

Forms

NET WORTH SHEET

THE FIVE LESSONS

AS OF _____
Date

ASSETS Current Liquid Assets

Cash (on hand)	$ _____
Checking Account	$ _____
Savings Account	$ _____
Certificates	$ _____
Money Owed You	$ _____
Tax Refund Due	$ _____
Life Insurance (Cash Value)	$ _____
Stocks/Bonds	$ _____
Mutual Fund Shares	$ _____
Precious Metals	$ _____
Other _____	$ _____
Other _____	$ _____
Total Current Assets	$ _____

FIXED ASSETS

Home	$ _____
Automobiles	$ _____
Furniture	$ _____
Jewelry	$ _____
Personal Property	$ _____
Other _____	$ _____
Total Fixed Assets	$ _____

DEFERRED ASSETS

Retirement Plan	$ _____
I.R.A.	$ _____
Other _____	$ _____
Other _____	$ _____
Total Deferred Assets	$ _____

TOTAL ASSETS $ _____

OTHER LIABILITIES Current Liabilities

Charge Accounts	$ _____
Credit Cards	$ _____
Insurance Due	$ _____
Taxes Due	$ _____
Current Bills Due	$ _____
Line of Credit	$ _____
Other _____	$ _____
Other _____	$ _____
Other _____	$ _____
Other _____	$ _____
Total Current Liabilities	$ _____

LONG-TERM LIABILITIES

Auto Loan #1	$ _____
Auto Loan #2	$ _____
Installment Loan	$ _____
Personal Loan	$ _____
Mortgage Loan	$ _____
Other _____	$ _____
Total Long-Term Liabilities	$ _____

TOTAL LIABILITIES $ _____

Total Assets	$ _____
Total Liabilities	$ _____
NET WORTH	$ _____

The Five Lessons a Millionaire Taught Me About Life and Wealth

For free copies of this form, visit our Web site at: thefivelessons.com.

THE FIVE
LESSONS

NET WORTH SHEET

AS OF _____
Date

ASSETS Current Liquid Assets

Cash (on hand)	$ _____
Checking Account	$ _____
Savings Account	$ _____
Certificates	$ _____
Money Owed You	$ _____
Tax Refund Due	$ _____
Life Insurance (Cash Value)	$ _____
Stocks/Bonds	$ _____
Mutual Fund Shares	$ _____
Precious Metals	$ _____
Other _____	$ _____
Other _____	$ _____
Total Current Assets	$ _____

FIXED ASSETS

Home	$ _____
Automobiles	$ _____
Furniture	$ _____
Jewelry	$ _____
Personal Property	$ _____
Other _____	$ _____
Total Fixed Assets	$ _____

DEFERRED ASSETS

Retirement Plan	$ _____
I.R.A.	$ _____
Other _____	$ _____
Other _____	$ _____
Total Deferred Assets	$ _____

TOTAL ASSETS $ _____

OTHERLIABILITIES Current Liabilities

Charge Accounts	$ _____
Credit Cards	$ _____
Insurance Due	$ _____
Taxes Due	$ _____
Current Bills Due	$ _____
Line of Credit	$ _____
Other _____	$ _____
Other _____	$ _____
Other _____	$ _____
Other _____	$ _____
Total Current Liabilities	$ _____

LONG-TERM LIABILITIES

Auto Loan #1	$ _____
Auto Loan #2	$ _____
Installment Loan	$ _____
Personal Loan	$ _____
Mortgage Loan	$ _____
Other _____	$ _____
Total Long-Term Liabilities	$ _____

TOTAL LIABILITIES $ _____

Total Assets	$ _____
Total Liabilities	$ _____
NET WORTH	$ _____

The Five Lessons a Millionaire Taught Me About Life and Wealth

For free copies of this form, visit our Web site at: thefivelessons.com.

THE FIVE LESSONS

NET WORTH SHEET

AS OF _____

Date

ASSETS Current Liquid Assets

Cash (on hand)	$ _____
Checking Account	$ _____
Savings Account	$ _____
Certificates	$ _____
Money Owed You	$ _____
Tax Refund Due	$ _____
Life Insurance (Cash Value)	$ _____
Stocks/Bonds	$ _____
Mutual Fund Shares	$ _____
Precious Metals	$ _____
Other _____	$ _____
Other _____	$ _____
Total Current Assets	$ _____

FIXED ASSETS

Home	$ _____
Automobiles	$ _____
Furniture	$ _____
Jewelry	$ _____
Personal Property	$ _____
Other _____	$ _____
Total Fixed Assets	$ _____

DEFERRED ASSETS

Retirement Plan	$ _____
I.R.A.	$ _____
Other _____	$ _____
Other _____	$ _____
Total Deferred Assets	$ _____

TOTAL ASSETS $ _____

OTHERLIABILITIES Current Liabilities

Charge Accounts	$ _____
Credit Cards	$ _____
Insurance Due	$ _____
Taxes Due	$ _____
Current Bills Due	$ _____
Line of Credit	$ _____
Other _____	$ _____
Other _____	$ _____
Other _____	$ _____
Other _____	$ _____
Total Current Liabilities	$ _____

LONG-TERM LIABILITIES

Auto Loan #1	$ _____
Auto Loan #2	$ _____
Installment Loan	$ _____
Personal Loan	$ _____
Mortgage Loan	$ _____
Other _____	$ _____
Total Long-Term Liabilities	$ _____

TOTAL LIABILITIES $ _____

Total Assets	$ _____
Total Liabilities	$ _____
NET WORTH	$ _____

The Five Lessons a Millionaire Taught Me About Life and Wealth

For free copies of this form, visit our Web site at: thefivelessons.com.

THE FIVE LESSONS

NET WORTH SHEET

AS OF _____
Date

ASSETS Current Liquid Assets

Cash (on hand)	$ _____
Checking Account	$ _____
Savings Account	$ _____
Certificates	$ _____
Money Owed You	$ _____
Tax Refund Due	$ _____
Life Insurance (Cash Value)	$ _____
Stocks/Bonds	$ _____
Mutual Fund Shares	$ _____
Precious Metals	$ _____
Other _____	$ _____
Other _____	$ _____
Total Current Assets	$ _____

FIXED ASSETS

Home	$ _____
Automobiles	$ _____
Furniture	$ _____
Jewelry	$ _____
Personal Property	$ _____
Other _____	$ _____
Total Fixed Assets	$ _____

DEFERRED ASSETS

Retirement Plan	$ _____
I.R.A.	$ _____
Other _____	$ _____
Other _____	$ _____
Total Deferred Assets	$ _____

TOTAL ASSETS $ _____

OTHER LIABILITIES Current Liabilities

Charge Accounts	$ _____
Credit Cards	$ _____
Insurance Due	$ _____
Taxes Due	$ _____
Current Bills Due	$ _____
Line of Credit	$ _____
Other _____	$ _____
Other _____	$ _____
Other _____	$ _____
Other _____	$ _____
Total Current Liabilities	$ _____

LONG-TERM LIABILITIES

Auto Loan #1	$ _____
Auto Loan #2	$ _____
Installment Loan	$ _____
Personal Loan	$ _____
Mortgage Loan	$ _____
Other _____	$ _____
Total Long-Term Liabilities	$ _____

TOTAL LIABILITIES $ _____

Total Assets	$ _____
Total Liabilities	$ _____
NET WORTH	$ _____

The Five Lessons a Millionaire Taught Me About Life and Wealth

For free copies of this form, visit our Web site at: thefivelessons.com.

NET WORTH SHEET

THE FIVE LESSONS

AS OF _____

Date

ASSETS Current Liquid Assets		**OTHER LIABILITIES** Current Liabilities	
Cash (on hand)	$ _____		
Checking Account	$ _____	Charge Accounts	$ _____
Savings Account	$ _____	Credit Cards	$ _____
Certificates	$ _____	Insurance Due	$ _____
Money Owed You	$ _____	Taxes Due	$ _____
Tax Refund Due	$ _____	Current Bills Due	$ _____
Life Insurance (Cash Value)	$ _____	Line of Credit	$ _____
Stocks/Bonds	$ _____	Other _____	$ _____
Mutual Fund Shares	$ _____	Other _____	$ _____
Precious Metals	$ _____	Other _____	$ _____
Other _____	$ _____	Other _____	$ _____
Other _____	$ _____		
Total Current Assets	$ _____	**Total Current Liabilities**	$ _____

FIXED ASSETS

LONG-TERM LIABILITIES

Home	$ _____	Auto Loan #1	$ _____
Automobiles	$ _____	Auto Loan #2	$ _____
Furniture	$ _____	Installment Loan	$ _____
Jewelry	$ _____	Personal Loan	$ _____
Personal Property	$ _____	Mortgage Loan	$ _____
Other _____	$ _____	Other _____	$ _____
Total Fixed Assets	$ _____	**Total Long-Term Liabilities**	$ _____

DEFERRED ASSETS

TOTAL LIABILITIES $ _____

Retirement Plan	$ _____
I.R.A.	$ _____
Other _____	$ _____
Other _____	$ _____
Total Deferred Assets	$ _____

Total Assets $ _____

Total Liabilities $ _____

NET WORTH $ _____

TOTAL ASSETS $ _____

The Five Lessons a Millionaire Taught Me About Life and Wealth

For free copies of this form, visit our Web site at: thefivelessons.com.

NET WORTH SHEET

THE FIVE LESSONS

AS OF _____
Date

ASSETS Current Liquid Assets		**OTHER LIABILITIES** Current Liabilities	
Cash (on hand)	$ _____		
Checking Account	$ _____	Charge Accounts	$ _____
Savings Account	$ _____	Credit Cards	$ _____
Certificates	$ _____	Insurance Due	$ _____
Money Owed You	$ _____	Taxes Due	$ _____
Tax Refund Due	$ _____	Current Bills Due	$ _____
Life Insurance (Cash Value)	$ _____	Line of Credit	$ _____
Stocks/Bonds	$ _____	Other _____	$ _____
Mutual Fund Shares	$ _____	Other _____	$ _____
Precious Metals	$ _____	Other _____	$ _____
Other _____	$ _____	Other _____	$ _____
Other _____	$ _____	**Total Current Liabilities**	$ _____
Total Current Assets	$ _____		

FIXED ASSETS		**LONG-TERM LIABILITIES**	
Home	$ _____	Auto Loan #1	$ _____
Automobiles	$ _____	Auto Loan #2	$ _____
Furniture	$ _____	Installment Loan	$ _____
Jewelry	$ _____	Personal Loan	$ _____
Personal Property	$ _____	Mortgage Loan	$ _____
Other _____	$ _____	Other _____	$ _____
Total Fixed Assets	$ _____	**Total Long-Term Liabilities**	$ _____

DEFERRED ASSETS		**TOTAL LIABILITIES**	$ _____
Retirement Plan	$ _____		
I.R.A.	$ _____		
Other _____	$ _____		
Other _____	$ _____		
Total Deferred Assets	$ _____		

Total Assets	$ _____
Total Liabilities	$ _____
NET WORTH	$ _____

TOTAL ASSETS $ _____

The Five Lessons a Millionaire Taught Me About Life and Wealth

For free copies of this form, visit our Web site at: thefivelessons.com.

NET WORTH SHEET

THE FIVE LESSONS

AS OF _____
Date

ASSETS Current Liquid Assets		OTHERLIABILITIES Current Liabilities	
Cash (on hand)	$ _____		
Checking Account	$ _____	Charge Accounts	$ _____
Savings Account	$ _____	Credit Cards	$ _____
Certificates	$ _____	Insurance Due	$ _____
Money Owed You	$ _____	Taxes Due	$ _____
Tax Refund Due	$ _____	Current Bills Due	$ _____
Life Insurance (Cash Value)	$ _____	Line of Credit	$ _____
Stocks/Bonds	$ _____	Other _____	$ _____
Mutual Fund Shares	$ _____	Other _____	$ _____
Precious Metals	$ _____	Other _____	$ _____
Other _____	$ _____	Other _____	$ _____
Other _____	$ _____		
		Total Current Liabilities	$ _____
Total Current Assets	$ _____		

FIXED ASSETS

LONG-TERM LIABILITIES

Home	$ _____	Auto Loan #1	$ _____
Automobiles	$ _____	Auto Loan #2	$ _____
Furniture	$ _____	Installment Loan	$ _____
Jewelry	$ _____	Personal Loan	$ _____
Personal Property	$ _____	Mortgage Loan	$ _____
Other _____	$ _____	Other _____	$ _____
		Total Long-Term Liabilities	$ _____
Total Fixed Assets	$ _____		

TOTAL LIABILITIES $ _____

DEFERRED ASSETS

Retirement Plan	$ _____	
I.R.A.	$ _____	
Other _____	$ _____	
Other _____	$ _____	
Total Deferred Assets	$ _____	

Total Assets $ _____
Total Liabilities $ _____
NET WORTH $ _____

TOTAL ASSETS $ _____

The Five Lessons a Millionaire Taught Me About Life and Wealth

For free copies of this form, visit our Web site at: thefivelessons.com.

NET WORTH SHEET

AS OF _____
Date

ASSETS Current Liquid Assets

Cash (on hand)	$ _____
Checking Account	$ _____
Savings Account	$ _____
Certificates	$ _____
Money Owed You	$ _____
Tax Refund Due	$ _____
Life Insurance (Cash Value)	$ _____
Stocks/Bonds	$ _____
Mutual Fund Shares	$ _____
Precious Metals	$ _____
Other _____	$ _____
Other _____	$ _____
Total Current Assets	$ _____

FIXED ASSETS

Home	$ _____
Automobiles	$ _____
Furniture	$ _____
Jewelry	$ _____
Personal Property	$ _____
Other _____	$ _____
Total Fixed Assets	$ _____

DEFERRED ASSETS

Retirement Plan	$ _____
I.R.A.	$ _____
Other _____	$ _____
Other _____	$ _____
Total Deferred Assets	$ _____

TOTAL ASSETS $ _____

OTHER LIABILITIES Current Liabilities

Charge Accounts	$ _____
Credit Cards	$ _____
Insurance Due	$ _____
Taxes Due	$ _____
Current Bills Due	$ _____
Line of Credit	$ _____
Other _____	$ _____
Other _____	$ _____
Other _____	$ _____
Other _____	$ _____
Total Current Liabilities	$ _____

LONG-TERM LIABILITIES

Auto Loan #1	$ _____
Auto Loan #2	$ _____
Installment Loan	$ _____
Personal Loan	$ _____
Mortgage Loan	$ _____
Other _____	$ _____
Total Long-Term Liabilities	$ _____

TOTAL LIABILITIES $ _____

Total Assets	$ _____
Total Liabilities	$ _____
NET WORTH	$ _____

The Five Lessons a Millionaire Taught Me About Life and Wealth

For free copies of this form, visit our Web site at: thefivelessons.com.

THE FIVE LESSONS

NET WORTH SHEET

AS OF _____
Date

ASSETS Current Liquid Assets

Cash (on hand)	$ _____
Checking Account	$ _____
Savings Account	$ _____
Certificates	$ _____
Money Owed You	$ _____
Tax Refund Due	$ _____
Life Insurance (Cash Value)	$ _____
Stocks/Bonds	$ _____
Mutual Fund Shares	$ _____
Precious Metals	$ _____
Other _____	$ _____
Other _____	$ _____
Total Current Assets	$ _____

FIXED ASSETS

Home	$ _____
Automobiles	$ _____
Furniture	$ _____
Jewelry	$ _____
Personal Property	$ _____
Other _____	$ _____
Total Fixed Assets	$ _____

DEFERRED ASSETS

Retirement Plan	$ _____
I.R.A.	$ _____
Other _____	$ _____
Other _____	$ _____
Total Deferred Assets	$ _____

TOTAL ASSETS $ _____

OTHER LIABILITIES Current Liabilities

Charge Accounts	$ _____
Credit Cards	$ _____
Insurance Due	$ _____
Taxes Due	$ _____
Current Bills Due	$ _____
Line of Credit	$ _____
Other _____	$ _____
Other _____	$ _____
Other _____	$ _____
Other _____	$ _____
Total Current Liabilities	$ _____

LONG-TERM LIABILITIES

Auto Loan #1	$ _____
Auto Loan #2	$ _____
Installment Loan	$ _____
Personal Loan	$ _____
Mortgage Loan	$ _____
Other _____	$ _____
Total Long-Term Liabilities	$ _____

TOTAL LIABILITIES $ _____

Total Assets	$ _____
Total Liabilities	$ _____
NET WORTH	$ _____

The Five Lessons a Millionaire Taught Me About Life and Wealth

For free copies of this form, visit our Web site at: thefivelessons.com.

NET WORTH SHEET

THE FIVE LESSONS

AS OF _____

Date

ASSETS Current Liquid Assets

Cash (on hand)	$ _____
Checking Account	$ _____
Savings Account	$ _____
Certificates	$ _____
Money Owed You	$ _____
Tax Refund Due	$ _____
Life Insurance (Cash Value)	$ _____
Stocks/Bonds	$ _____
Mutual Fund Shares	$ _____
Precious Metals	$ _____
Other _____	$ _____
Other _____	$ _____
Total Current Assets	$ _____

FIXED ASSETS

Home	$ _____
Automobiles	$ _____
Furniture	$ _____
Jewelry	$ _____
Personal Property	$ _____
Other _____	$ _____
Total Fixed Assets	$ _____

DEFERRED ASSETS

Retirement Plan	$ _____
I.R.A.	$ _____
Other _____	$ _____
Other _____	$ _____
Total Deferred Assets	$ _____

TOTAL ASSETS $ _____

OTHERLIABILITIES Current Liabilities

Charge Accounts	$ _____
Credit Cards	$ _____
Insurance Due	$ _____
Taxes Due	$ _____
Current Bills Due	$ _____
Line of Credit	$ _____
Other _____	$ _____
Other _____	$ _____
Other _____	$ _____
Other _____	$ _____
Total Current Liabilities	$ _____

LONG-TERM LIABILITIES

Auto Loan #1	$ _____
Auto Loan #2	$ _____
Installment Loan	$ _____
Personal Loan	$ _____
Mortgage Loan	$ _____
Other _____	$ _____
Total Long-Term Liabilities	$ _____

TOTAL LIABILITIES $ _____

Total Assets	$ _____
Total Liabilities	$ _____
NET WORTH	$ _____

The Five Lessons a Millionaire Taught Me About Life and Wealth

For free copies of this form, visit our Web site at: thefivelessons.com.

NET WORTH SHEET

THE FIVE LESSONS

AS OF _____
Date

ASSETS Current Liquid Assets		OTHERLIABILITIES Current Liabilities	
Cash (on hand)	$ _____		
Checking Account	$ _____	Charge Accounts	$ _____
Savings Account	$ _____	Credit Cards	$ _____
Certificates	$ _____	Insurance Due	$ _____
Money Owed You	$ _____	Taxes Due	$ _____
Tax Refund Due	$ _____	Current Bills Due	$ _____
Life Insurance (Cash Value)	$ _____	Line of Credit	$ _____
Stocks/Bonds	$ _____	Other _____	$ _____
Mutual Fund Shares	$ _____	Other _____	$ _____
Precious Metals	$ _____	Other _____	$ _____
Other _____	$ _____	Other _____	$ _____
Other _____	$ _____		
Total Current Assets	$ _____	**Total Current Liabilities**	$ _____

FIXED ASSETS

LONG-TERM LIABILITIES

Home	$ _____	Auto Loan #1	$ _____
Automobiles	$ _____	Auto Loan #2	$ _____
Furniture	$ _____	Installment Loan	$ _____
Jewelry	$ _____	Personal Loan	$ _____
Personal Property	$ _____	Mortgage Loan	$ _____
Other _____	$ _____	Other _____	$ _____
Total Fixed Assets	$ _____	**Total Long-Term Liabilities**	$ _____

DEFERRED ASSETS

TOTAL LIABILITIES $ _____

Retirement Plan	$ _____	
I.R.A.	$ _____	
Other _____	$ _____	
Other _____	$ _____	
Total Deferred Assets	$ _____	

Total Assets	$ _____
Total Liabilities	$ _____
NET WORTH	$ _____

TOTAL ASSETS $ _____

The Five Lessons a Millionaire Taught Me About Life and Wealth

For free copies of this form, visit our Web site at: thefivelessons.com.

NET WORTH SHEET

THE FIVE LESSONS

AS OF _____
Date

ASSETS Current Liquid Assets		**OTHERLIABILITIES** Current Liabilities	
Cash (on hand)	$ _____		
Checking Account	$ _____	Charge Accounts	$ _____
Savings Account	$ _____	Credit Cards	$ _____
Certificates	$ _____	Insurance Due	$ _____
Money Owed You	$ _____	Taxes Due	$ _____
Tax Refund Due	$ _____	Current Bills Due	$ _____
Life Insurance (Cash Value)	$ _____	Line of Credit	$ _____
Stocks/Bonds	$ _____	Other _____	$ _____
Mutual Fund Shares	$ _____	Other _____	$ _____
Precious Metals	$ _____	Other _____	$ _____
Other _____	$ _____	Other _____	$ _____
Other _____	$ _____		
		Total Current Liabilities	$ _____
Total Current Assets	$ _____		
		LONG-TERM LIABILITIES	
FIXED ASSETS		Auto Loan #1	$ _____
Home	$ _____	Auto Loan #2	$ _____
Automobiles	$ _____	Installment Loan	$ _____
Furniture	$ _____	Personal Loan	$ _____
Jewelry	$ _____	Mortgage Loan	$ _____
Personal Property	$ _____	Other _____	$ _____
Other _____	$ _____		
		Total Long-Term Liabilities	$ _____
Total Fixed Assets	$ _____		
		TOTAL LIABILITIES	$ _____
DEFERRED ASSETS			
Retirement Plan	$ _____		
I.R.A.	$ _____		
Other _____	$ _____		
Other _____	$ _____		

Total Assets $ _____

Total Liabilities $ _____

NET WORTH $ _____

Total Deferred Assets $ _____

TOTAL ASSETS $ _____   *The Five Lessons a Millionaire Taught Me About Life and Wealth*

For free copies of this form, visit our Web site at: thefivelessons.com.

THE FIVE LESSONS

CASH FLOW SHEET

CASH FLOW FOR _____

Date

INCOME	Planned	Actual
Salary 1 (after taxes)	$ _____	$ _____
Salary 2 (after taxes)	$ _____	$ _____
Other Income	$ _____	$ _____
Other Income	$ _____	$ _____
Total Income	$ _____	$ _____

EXPENDITURES		
Nest Egg *(min. 10% of total income)*	$ _____	$ _____
Charitable Donations	$ _____	$ _____
Mortgage or Rent	$ _____	$ _____
Food	$ _____	$ _____
Utilities	$ _____	$ _____
Auto Payments	$ _____	$ _____
Misc. Auto Expense	$ _____	$ _____
Repair	$ _____	$ _____
Maintenance	$ _____	$ _____
Gas	$ _____	$ _____
Auto Insurance	$ _____	$ _____
Life Insurance	$ _____	$ _____
Home Owner's Insurance	$ _____	$ _____
Medical Insurance	$ _____	$ _____
Clothing	$ _____	$ _____
Debt Payments	$ _____	$ _____
Misc. Expenses	$ _____	$ _____
TOTAL EXPENDITURES	$ _____	$ _____
Income Less Expenditures	$ _____	$ _____

The Five Lessons a Millionaire Taught Me About Life and Wealth

For free copies of this form, visit our Web site at: thefivelessons.com.

THE FIVE LESSONS

CASH FLOW SHEET

CASH FLOW FOR _____

Date

INCOME	Planned	Actual
Salary 1 (after taxes)	$	$
Salary 2 (after taxes)	$	$
Other Income	$	$
Other Income	$	$
Total Income	$	$

EXPENDITURES		
Nest Egg *(min. 10% of total income)*	$	$
Charitable Donations	$	$
Mortgage or Rent	$	$
Food	$	$
Utilities	$	$
Auto Payments	$	$
Misc. Auto Expense	$	$
Repair	$	$
Maintenance	$	$
Gas	$	$
Auto Insurance	$	$
Life Insurance	$	$
Home Owner's Insurance	$	$
Medical Insurance	$	$
Clothing	$	$
Debt Payments	$	$
Misc. Expenses	$	$
TOTAL EXPENDITURES	$	$
Income Less Expenditures	$	$

The Five Lessons a Millionaire Taught Me About Life and Wealth

For free copies of this form, visit our Web site at: thefivelessons.com.

CASH FLOW SHEET

THE FIVE LESSONS

CASH FLOW FOR _____

Date

INCOME	Planned	Actual
Salary 1 (after taxes)	$ _____	$ _____
Salary 2 (after taxes)	$ _____	$ _____
Other Income	$ _____	$ _____
Other Income	$ _____	$ _____
Total Income	$ _____	$ _____

EXPENDITURES		
Nest Egg (*min. 10% of total income*)	$ _____	$ _____
Charitable Donations	$ _____	$ _____
Mortgage or Rent	$ _____	$ _____
Food	$ _____	$ _____
Utilities	$ _____	$ _____
Auto Payments	$ _____	$ _____
Misc. Auto Expense	$ _____	$ _____
Repair	$ _____	$ _____
Maintenance	$ _____	$ _____
Gas	$ _____	$ _____
Auto Insurance	$ _____	$ _____
Life Insurance	$ _____	$ _____
Home Owner's Insurance	$ _____	$ _____
Medical Insurance	$ _____	$ _____
Clothing	$ _____	$ _____
Debt Payments	$ _____	$ _____
Misc. Expenses	$ _____	$ _____
TOTAL EXPENDITURES	$ _____	$ _____
Income Less Expenditures	$ _____	$ _____

The Five Lessons a Millionaire Taught Me About Life and Wealth

For free copies of this form, visit our Web site at: thefivelessons.com.

CASH FLOW SHEET

THE FIVE LESSONS

CASH FLOW FOR _____
Date

INCOME	Planned	Actual
Salary 1 (after taxes)	$ _____	$ _____
Salary 2 (after taxes)	$ _____	$ _____
Other Income	$ _____	$ _____
Other Income	$ _____	$ _____
Total Income	$ _____	$ _____

EXPENDITURES

Nest Egg *(min. 10% of total income)*	$ _____	$ _____
Charitable Donations	$ _____	$ _____
Mortgage or Rent	$ _____	$ _____
Food	$ _____	$ _____
Utilities	$ _____	$ _____
Auto Payments	$ _____	$ _____
Misc. Auto Expense	$ _____	$ _____
Repair	$ _____	$ _____
Maintenance	$ _____	$ _____
Gas	$ _____	$ _____
Auto Insurance	$ _____	$ _____
Life Insurance	$ _____	$ _____
Home Owner's Insurance	$ _____	$ _____
Medical Insurance	$ _____	$ _____
Clothing	$ _____	$ _____
Debt Payments	$ _____	$ _____
Misc. Expenses	$ _____	$ _____
TOTAL EXPENDITURES	$ _____	$ _____
Income Less Expenditures	$ _____	$ _____

The Five Lessons a Millionaire Taught Me About Life and Wealth

For free copies of this form, visit our Web site at: thefivelessons.com.

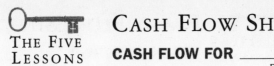

CASH FLOW SHEET

THE FIVE LESSONS

CASH FLOW FOR _____
Date

INCOME	Planned	Actual
Salary 1 (after taxes)	$	$
Salary 2 (after taxes)	$	$
Other Income	$	$
Other Income	$	$
Total Income	$	$

EXPENDITURES		
Nest Egg (*min. 10% of total income*)	$	$
Charitable Donations	$	$
Mortgage or Rent	$	$
Food	$	$
Utilities	$	$
Auto Payments	$	$
Misc. Auto Expense	$	$
Repair	$	$
Maintenance	$	$
Gas	$	$
Auto Insurance	$	$
Life Insurance	$	$
Home Owner's Insurance	$	$
Medical Insurance	$	$
Clothing	$	$
Debt Payments	$	$
Misc. Expenses	$	$

TOTAL EXPENDITURES	$	$
Income Less Expenditures	$	$

The Five Lessons a Millionaire Taught Me About Life and Wealth

For free copies of this form, visit our Web site at: thefivelessons.com.

CASH FLOW SHEET

THE FIVE
LESSONS

CASH FLOW FOR _____
Date

INCOME	Planned	Actual
Salary 1 (after taxes)	$ _____	$ _____
Salary 2 (after taxes)	$ _____	$ _____
Other Income	$ _____	$ _____
Other Income	$ _____	$ _____
Total Income	$ _____	$ _____

EXPENDITURES

	Planned	Actual
Nest Egg *(min. 10% of total income)*	$ _____	$ _____
Charitable Donations	$ _____	$ _____
Mortgage or Rent	$ _____	$ _____
Food	$ _____	$ _____
Utilities	$ _____	$ _____
Auto Payments	$ _____	$ _____
Misc. Auto Expense	$ _____	$ _____
Repair	$ _____	$ _____
Maintenance	$ _____	$ _____
Gas	$ _____	$ _____
Auto Insurance	$ _____	$ _____
Life Insurance	$ _____	$ _____
Home Owner's Insurance	$ _____	$ _____
Medical Insurance	$ _____	$ _____
Clothing	$ _____	$ _____
Debt Payments	$ _____	$ _____
Misc. Expenses	$ _____	$ _____
TOTAL EXPENDITURES	$ _____	$ _____
Income Less Expenditures	$ _____	$ _____

The Five Lessons a Millionaire Taught Me About Life and Wealth

For free copies of this form, visit our Web site at: thefivelessons.com.

THE FIVE LESSONS

CASH FLOW SHEET

CASH FLOW FOR _____
Date

INCOME	Planned	Actual
Salary 1 (after taxes)	$ _____	$ _____
Salary 2 (after taxes)	$ _____	$ _____
Other Income	$ _____	$ _____
Other Income	$ _____	$ _____
Total Income	$ _____	$ _____

EXPENDITURES		
Nest Egg *(min. 10% of total income)*	$ _____	$ _____
Charitable Donations	$ _____	$ _____
Mortgage or Rent	$ _____	$ _____
Food	$ _____	$ _____
Utilities	$ _____	$ _____
Auto Payments	$ _____	$ _____
Misc. Auto Expense	$ _____	$ _____
Repair	$ _____	$ _____
Maintenance	$ _____	$ _____
Gas	$ _____	$ _____
Auto Insurance	$ _____	$ _____
Life Insurance	$ _____	$ _____
Home Owner's Insurance	$ _____	$ _____
Medical Insurance	$ _____	$ _____
Clothing	$ _____	$ _____
Debt Payments	$ _____	$ _____
Misc. Expenses	$ _____	$ _____

TOTAL EXPENDITURES	$ _____	$ _____
Income Less Expenditures	$ _____	$ _____

The Five Lessons a Millionaire Taught Me About Life and Wealth

For free copies of this form, visit our Web site at: thefivelessons.com.

THE FIVE LESSONS

CASH FLOW SHEET

CASH FLOW FOR _____
Date

INCOME	Planned	Actual
Salary 1 (after taxes)	$ _____	$ _____
Salary 2 (after taxes)	$ _____	$ _____
Other Income	$ _____	$ _____
Other Income	$ _____	$ _____
Total Income	$ _____	$ _____

EXPENDITURES		
Nest Egg (*min. 10% of total income*)	$ _____	$ _____
Charitable Donations	$ _____	$ _____
Mortgage or Rent	$ _____	$ _____
Food	$ _____	$ _____
Utilities	$ _____	$ _____
Auto Payments	$ _____	$ _____
Misc. Auto Expense	$ _____	$ _____
Repair	$ _____	$ _____
Maintenance	$ _____	$ _____
Gas	$ _____	$ _____
Auto Insurance	$ _____	$ _____
Life Insurance	$ _____	$ _____
Home Owner's Insurance	$ _____	$ _____
Medical Insurance	$ _____	$ _____
Clothing	$ _____	$ _____
Debt Payments	$ _____	$ _____
Misc. Expenses	$ _____	$ _____

TOTAL EXPENDITURES	$ _____	$ _____
Income Less Expenditures	$ _____	$ _____

The Five Lessons a Millionaire Taught Me About Life and Wealth

For free copies of this form, visit our Web site at: thefivelessons.com.

THE FIVE LESSONS

CASH FLOW SHEET

CASH FLOW FOR _____
Date

INCOME	Planned	Actual
Salary 1 (after taxes)	$ _____	$ _____
Salary 2 (after taxes)	$ _____	$ _____
Other Income	$ _____	$ _____
Other Income	$ _____	$ _____
Total Income	$ _____	$ _____

EXPENDITURES

	Planned	Actual
Nest Egg (*min. 10% of total income*)	$ _____	$ _____
Charitable Donations	$ _____	$ _____
Mortgage or Rent	$ _____	$ _____
Food	$ _____	$ _____
Utilities	$ _____	$ _____
Auto Payments	$ _____	$ _____
Misc. Auto Expense	$ _____	$ _____
Repair	$ _____	$ _____
Maintenance	$ _____	$ _____
Gas	$ _____	$ _____
Auto Insurance	$ _____	$ _____
Life Insurance	$ _____	$ _____
Home Owner's Insurance	$ _____	$ _____
Medical Insurance	$ _____	$ _____
Clothing	$ _____	$ _____
Debt Payments	$ _____	$ _____
Misc. Expenses	$ _____	$ _____
TOTAL EXPENDITURES	$ _____	$ _____
Income Less Expenditures	$ _____	$ _____

The Five Lessons a Millionaire Taught Me About Life and Wealth

For free copies of this form, visit our Web site at: thefivelessons.com.

THE FIVE LESSONS

CASH FLOW SHEET

CASH FLOW FOR _____
Date

INCOME	Planned	Actual
Salary 1 (after taxes)	$ _____	$ _____
Salary 2 (after taxes)	$ _____	$ _____
Other Income	$ _____	$ _____
Other Income	$ _____	$ _____
Total Income	$ _____	$ _____

EXPENDITURES		
Nest Egg *(min. 10% of total income)*	$ _____	$ _____
Charitable Donations	$ _____	$ _____
Mortgage or Rent	$ _____	$ _____
Food	$ _____	$ _____
Utilities	$ _____	$ _____
Auto Payments	$ _____	$ _____
Misc. Auto Expense	$ _____	$ _____
Repair	$ _____	$ _____
Maintenance	$ _____	$ _____
Gas	$ _____	$ _____
Auto Insurance	$ _____	$ _____
Life Insurance	$ _____	$ _____
Home Owner's Insurance	$ _____	$ _____
Medical Insurance	$ _____	$ _____
Clothing	$ _____	$ _____
Debt Payments	$ _____	$ _____
Misc. Expenses	$ _____	$ _____
TOTAL EXPENDITURES	$ _____	$ _____
Income Less Expenditures	$ _____	$ _____

The Five Lessons a Millionaire Taught Me About Life and Wealth

For free copies of this form, visit our Web site at: thefivelessons.com.

CASH FLOW SHEET

THE FIVE LESSONS

CASH FLOW FOR _____
Date

INCOME	Planned	Actual
Salary 1 (after taxes)	$ _____	$ _____
Salary 2 (after taxes)	$ _____	$ _____
Other Income	$ _____	$ _____
Other Income	$ _____	$ _____
Total Income	$ _____	$ _____

EXPENDITURES		
Nest Egg (*min. 10% of total income*)	$ _____	$ _____
Charitable Donations	$ _____	$ _____
Mortgage or Rent	$ _____	$ _____
Food	$ _____	$ _____
Utilities	$ _____	$ _____
Auto Payments	$ _____	$ _____
Misc. Auto Expense	$ _____	$ _____
Repair	$ _____	$ _____
Maintenance	$ _____	$ _____
Gas	$ _____	$ _____
Auto Insurance	$ _____	$ _____
Life Insurance	$ _____	$ _____
Home Owner's Insurance	$ _____	$ _____
Medical Insurance	$ _____	$ _____
Clothing	$ _____	$ _____
Debt Payments	$ _____	$ _____
Misc. Expenses	$ _____	$ _____

TOTAL EXPENDITURES $ _____ $ _____

Income Less Expenditures $ _____ $ _____

The Five Lessons a Millionaire Taught Me About Life and Wealth

For free copies of this form, visit our Web site at: thefivelessons.com.

THE FIVE LESSONS

CASH FLOW SHEET

CASH FLOW FOR _____
Date

INCOME	Planned	Actual
Salary 1 (after taxes)	$ _____	$ _____
Salary 2 (after taxes)	$ _____	$ _____
Other Income	$ _____	$ _____
Other Income	$ _____	$ _____
Total Income	$ _____	$ _____

EXPENDITURES		
Nest Egg (*min. 10% of total income*)	$ _____	$ _____
Charitable Donations	$ _____	$ _____
Mortgage or Rent	$ _____	$ _____
Food	$ _____	$ _____
Utilities	$ _____	$ _____
Auto Payments	$ _____	$ _____
Misc. Auto Expense	$ _____	$ _____
Repair	$ _____	$ _____
Maintenance	$ _____	$ _____
Gas	$ _____	$ _____
Auto Insurance	$ _____	$ _____
Life Insurance	$ _____	$ _____
Home Owner's Insurance	$ _____	$ _____
Medical Insurance	$ _____	$ _____
Clothing	$ _____	$ _____
Debt Payments	$ _____	$ _____
Misc. Expenses	$ _____	$ _____
TOTAL EXPENDITURES	$ _____	$ _____
Income Less Expenditures	$ _____	$ _____

The Five Lessons a Millionaire Taught Me About Life and Wealth

For free copies of this form, visit our Web site at: thefivelessons.com.

JOIN THE FIVE LESSONS REVOLUTION!

To join the *Five Lessons* mailing list and receive a FREE monthly newsletter, download free financial forms, or find the next *Five Lessons* seminar in your area, go to Richard's Web site at:

www.thefivelessons.com.

Please send correspondence to:

Richard@thefivelessons.com

Please send mail to:

Richard Paul Evans
P.O. Box 1416
Salt Lake City, Utah 84110

ABOUT THE AUTHOR

RICHARD PAUL EVANS is the author of nine *New York Times* best-selling novels and five children's books. He has won the American Mothers' Book Award and two first-place Storytelling World Awards for his children's books. His books have been translated into more than eighteen languages. More than thirteen million copies of his books are in print worldwide. *Newsweek* and *The Washington Post* have noted his business skills. At the age of thirty he was the recipient of the Ernst & Young Entrepreneur of the Year Lifetime Achievement Award. He is also the founder of the Christmas Box House International, an organization dedicated to helping abused and neglected children. More than sixteen thousand children have been housed in Christmas Box Houses. He is the recipient of the *Washington Times* Humanitarian of the Century Award and the Volunteers of America Empathy Award. He lives in Salt Lake City, Utah, with his wife and their five children.